A WORLD APART

By the same author

LOVE UNTIL IT HURTS
(published by Hodder & Stoughton, 1981)

A WORLD APART

Daphne Rae

with line drawings by Jean Harper

LUTTERWORTH PRESS
Guildford Surrey England

Copyright © 1983 by Daphne Rae

ISBN 0–7188–2558–6

Typeset in 10½ on 12 point Bembo
by Nene Phototypesetters Ltd, Northampton
Printed and bound in Great Britain
by Mackays of Chatham Ltd

CONTENTS

To
BOBBIE JAMES
to add to her memories of Jimmy
to whom,
and her,
we owe so much

AUTHOR'S ACKNOWLEDGEMENTS

First and foremost, my gratitude to John for his encouragement and to the children for putting up with it all.

Many people have helped towards the production of this book, and I would like to thank all of them. Some names which come to mind are: Bruce Blair, Edgar Bradley, Cedric Bush, Edward Carpenter, Hilary Dean, Edward England, James Fox, Michael Foxell, John Grigg, Patrick Lichfield, Paul Wigmore, and Anthea Morton-Saner – but there are many others.

I am particularly grateful to Lord Longford who encouraged me from the first, offered to write a foreword if and when the manuscript was completed, and has made good his word with characteristic kindness.

There are two people who deserve my deepest gratitude. One is my old friend Jean Harper whose work I greatly admire. I was delighted that she agreed to do the drawings which add so much to the book. The other is Jenny Overton – my editor. Edward England once said that the relationship between author and editor resembles that between anxious mother and obstetrician – I am happy to report that delivery was successful, without trauma to either party, and in fact thoroughly enjoyable.

The friends and colleagues whom we first met at Harrow, under the wise headmastership of Jimmy James, made our days there a very happy period of our lives. I hope that our old friend Ian Beer, who is now Head Master, and his wife Angela, will find as much happiness at the school as was given to us during our eleven years there.

EDITOR'S ACKNOWLEDGEMENTS

Brief quotations from printed and manuscript sources are given in quotation marks, with the author's name, the title and the date of publication cited in the course of the passage.

Longer quotations are set in smaller type and carry a source note number. They may be identified from the list of sources on page 178.

The author and her publishers would like to thank all those who have granted permission for the quoting of copyright material in this book, in particular the following:

Methuen London for the quotations from *Paint and Prejudice* by C. R. Nevinson (1937);

John Murray (Publishers) Ltd for the quotations from *In My Hot Youth*, from Volume I of *Byron's Letters and Journals* (1973) edited by Leslie A. Marchand;

Methuen London for the quotations from *Come What May* by Arnold Lunn (1940);

Hollis and Carter at the Bodley Head for the quotation from *Eton* by Christopher Hollis (1960);

Dr Ismond Rosen and Oxford University Press for the quotation from *Sexual Deviation* (1979);

Faber & Faber for the quotation from *Public School Religion* by Arnold Lunn and other authors (1933);

The Hamlyn Publishing Group Ltd for the quotation from *My Early Life* by Winston Churchill, originally published by Odhams Press Ltd (1930);

Dr John Rae and *Punch* for the article on success published on March 11, 1981.

FOREWORD
by Lord Longford

Daphne Rae has written a penetrating and most entertaining book.
Wife of the Head Master of Westminster, who was previously an
assistant master at Harrow and Head Master of Taunton, she
knows from close at hand the strength and weaknesses of our
public schools. Her book is full of delicious anecdotes. This is one
of my favourites: a well-qualified candidate for a headmastership
appeared before a Governing Body. The Chairman, an elderly
bishop, asked him: 'I have been looking through your curriculum
vitae, but I see no mention of the games you play, although I
understand you believe games are an important part of the school
timetable. What games, Sir, have you played?'

'Cricket,' my friend replied cheerfully.

'Ah, good. Were you Captain of the Eleven at Winchester?'

'Oh no, I was not in *the* team.'

'Second Eleven, perhaps?'

'No – I played twice for the Fourth Eleven.'

There was an audible intake of breath. The silence was intense.
The eyes looked anywhere but at the applicant. The bishop
swallowed.

'Twice for the Fourth Eleven?' he asked incredulously. He pondered, and a thought came to him. Raising his head, he continued:

'Ah, but you are still young. With practice you may improve.'

The candidate, a Wykehamist, rose to his feet. 'Good afternoon,
gentlemen – I must return to my sixth form.'

Daphne Rae adds a characteristic touch. 'The successful applicant lasted four years, before being asked to leave.'

Some of her best stories derive from the fanatical enthusiasm for winning at games, so prevalent in public schools. I will add one of my own. I played against Harrow in their first match after taking up rugger. With a minute to go, we were leading by two points and Harrow seemed certain to lose. But their coach, an old Irish international who was playing for us, had other ideas. He lurked about, obviously off-side, till penalised by the referee, the famous Potter-Irwin. 'Caught me that time, Potter old man,' he remarked genially, and showed high elation when the inevitable penalty goal was kicked and Harrow won their first match.

Daphne Rae describes herself as having become an old hand at being a rugger spectator. She says she felt quite at home surrounded by masters and their families, and hundreds of boys eager to cheer. But some of her reflections were probably shared by few of her companions. 'Was I to join the hearty "hallo there" group of adolescent adults, whose personalities were transformed by the very mention of any sport? I stood glassy-eyed and trembling to think that in twenty years' time, I might be standing on the same spot watching a future generation playing on the same pitch, and holding a fixture list with the names of the same public schools.'

I picture her as a most beneficent influence wherever she found herself, but she does not exclude the other side of her life. The last paragraph of the book must be quoted in full: 'Headmastering at Taunton and Westminster has increased our loneliness. We have fewer friends and more acquaintances, and the pressures of a largely artificial existence led me to work first among the terminally ill in this country and then among the dying and destitute overseas.

'But that – together with my further experiences as a headmaster's wife – is another story.'

A remarkable book, by a remarkable woman.

Introduction

In my light-hearted way I planned to write a series of anecdotes about Harrow School from the point of view of a schoolmaster's wife. It was to be a personal account of incidents and intrigues which I had experienced, but I also wanted to enlarge on the more serious problems of life in enclosed single-sex communities. I thought that if my family had nothing better to do, they might browse through my poorly-typed pages and share some of the memories; laugh at the ridiculous moments, and argue over my psychological theories.

When I finished the first draft, I gave it to my husband, and left him for the afternoon. On my return, he was practically in tears with laughter.

'I have only added two paragraphs to enlarge on the fact that it was because I was a hypochondriac that I obtained my first headmastership,' he said (a story told in full in this book). 'You must get this printed,' he laughed, 'I don't think a public-school story has been told by the wife of a master.'

He persuaded me to approach a firm of publishers. I had just produced a book on working in India, so I was not entirely green as far as the publishing world was concerned. Nevertheless I was pleasantly surprised by the kindness I received. They said how much they enjoyed the book, made various suggestions, and did everything but publish it.

'We have no "slot" to put it into: you touch on education, psychology, morals and biography,' they said, and then added, 'We would like you to enlarge on the biography.'

I reluctantly took their advice, for I could not believe that anyone would be interested in my past life – strange and bizarre though it had been, very much a world apart. Although they did not become its eventual publishers, the book in its present form owes much to their early advice and encouragement; the opinions remain my own.

In February 1982, before leaving for India, I sent a copy of the new draft to one publisher, and by mistake my agent at the same time sent a copy to another. On my return I was dumbfounded to find that both publishers wished to offer for the manuscript. I am grateful to them for a gesture of such encouragement. An agreement was concluded with Lutterworth Press, and this book was the result.

Childhood

'Hallo darling, I am at the Head Master's, and we've just had dinner. I think the hierarchy might be afraid of homosexuality, as they prefer married men on the staff. There is an old condemned cottage in the Sanatorium grounds, which is empty, it's been suggested that we might get married at Christmas. How about it? You must give me an answer now, as the coffee and liqueurs are being served in the drawing-room, and I told them that I'd have a reply.'

It was one of the rare occasions in my life when I was at a loss for words. My clammy hand held the telephone, and I stuttered:

'But Christmas is only six weeks away.'

'I know,' he said. I was silent. 'Are you OK?'

'Yes, I'm OK,' I replied feebly.

'Good, Christmas then – I'll go and tell them – cheers!'

What on earth had I done? I had just committed myself for life by saying, 'I'm OK.' I certainly didn't feel OK. No doubt John was the centre of attention in the Head Master's black-carpeted drawing-room, surrounded by dinner-jacketed fellow guests. I remained rooted to the floor, the burring telephone clutched tightly in my hand. In my mind I could hear the 'Congratulations, old boy' and the hollow sound of his back being thumped. I could picture glasses being raised to toast the health of this young 'beak' who, fresh from Cambridge, had been a master at Harrow School for precisely six weeks. I felt very alone. It was too late to

1

'phone my friends, and anyway I would be incoherent, so I did what I always do under stress. I went and sat in a warm bath and thought of the past, cringed at the present, and made plans for the future.

★ ★ ★

I was born on August 15, 1933, in the Gaulle Face Nursing Home, Colombo, Ceylon, which has now been renamed Sri Lanka. My address was more romantic than my birth. I have since been told that my entry into society was long and painful. The screams from the labour ward were horrific, and the doctor had his shirt torn by the frightened and angry patient. At last the child was born. After the months of discomfort and the indignity of labour, a well-formed nine-pounder greeted the mother face to face. It was the final insult, for I turned out to be a girl.

I have a photograph of my father holding me, within hours of my birth. I am naked, but round my middle – no doubt to hide the umbilical cord – is a large pink satin ribbon. He, at least, accepted me.

. My first years were spent in the care of an ayah. She was protective and patient: did she introduce me to the Indian way of life that I love so much? She moulded me in my first years. It was she who taught me to walk, talk and swim. She spent hours taking me for walks and playing games with me. She was my pillar of strength. I remember having showers with her, when she would stand on the tiled floor dressed in a white, widow's robe which clung to her not-so-young body while she washed my fair curly hair. (White, not black, is the colour of mourning in the East.) I always wore the most beautiful hand-made clothes which she changed at least twice a day. On occasions I would be paraded in front of guests, but Ayah was always close by to whisk me off to other quarters as soon as it was polite to do so.

When I try to remember my parents together, my recollections are not particularly happy. I recall a lot of noise – arguments and shouting. Ayah would rush into the room, pick me up in her arms and take me away. She sheltered me from unnecessary abuse and at their parties was quick to remove me from alcoholic adults, for even at that age I was well aware of the after-effects of too much drink.

There was a magical period when my mother was not there. I rode on a small elephant at the waterside near Mount Lavinia

Hotel, where the trees cast long shadows, and the beach below beckoned invitingly. I remember the swirling currents which lapped gently onto the sands, the monkeys making merry in the branches and the highly-coloured tropical birds casually calling us all to join in their freedom. The songs, the smells, the colours lodged in my memory. Indian craftsmen were working at their stalls, which fringed the road leading up to the hotel. One particular man would expertly reshape gold coins into charms. I still have a dog and an elephant which he made for me at the request of my father.

Then suddenly my mother appeared again, and my existence was shattered. Gone were the days of Ayah's loving arms and tender soft voice, the warm sea and the sun-drenched beaches. Gone was my father, never to be seen again by me.

I was dragged away screaming from my much-loved and kind Ayah. It happened so suddenly and without warning. Ayah and I returned from a walk on the beach and she was instructed to pack my clothes immediately as I was leaving for England. My whole world was torn apart. Ayah was in tears. I clung to her as she sorted out my belongings.

In vain I searched the house for my father. He had not been told of our departure. Those that I loved I would never see again. I had doted on my gentle giant of a father who had invariably shown me love and kindness and on whose strong broad shoulders I had proudly sat and viewed the countryside. From that day I became independent.

I wonder whether it was fear or shock that made me devious at the early age of four. Lonely and terrified on the P. and O. liner which set sail from Colombo to England, unable to speak without tears, I pretended that I could not understand English well, and remained silent. I rarely saw my mother on that long journey. I recall being involved with other children on board – obviously in a playroom for children – and I attached myself to some other ayah. I vaguely recollect a swimming-pool.

England was cold. We went to stay with my mother's Aunt Maud and her husband, a doctor in Cheshire. Large and red-faced with strange, protruding ice-blue eyes, he was very different from the romantic ideal of a country general practitioner. 'No one would ever believe half of what you say about him,' stated a distant relation who read this story. 'He should have been struck off the Medical Register and put into prison.' We called him

3

'U.B.', short for Uncle Bob, and his wife, Aunt Maud, was 'A.M.'. They were a childless couple. Soon my mother went away, leaving me there with U.B. and A.M. as my official guardians. I was to stay with them during my school holidays for the next eight years, unless I was fortunate enough to be invited to stay with school friends instead. I was still only four years old when I went to my first boarding-school.

Their home was a large white house, run by Irish maids. When the girls landed at Liverpool after crossing the Irish Sea, and told the immigration authorities where they were going to work, they were warned that their future employer was not to be trusted. 'He's got wandering hands, Miss Daphne,' they said, giggling, when I asked them why they would jump and upset the soup as they served him at table. 'You'd think he would be satisfied enough after his surgeries – but this dirty old man has only to see a female's leg, and his hand dives up it.' They worked hard, those maids, and remained cheerful.

Aunt Maud was a superior soul. She saw what happened and pretended that it didn't. She prayed that U.B. would be forgiven, and that she would be granted the strength to accept his faults and forget them. She was frightened of him and with reason. Her alcoholic mother had been widowed and came over from Ireland to stay with Aunt Maud, her eldest child. Soon after her arrival, she fell down some stone steps leading from the garden to the house. Her leg was obviously broken, and she was taken up to her bedroom by the chauffeur. When U.B. went to see her, he found her distressed and in pain. He refused to give her any treatment, or to set the leg, until a solicitor was called from Manchester, several miles away. His mother-in-law had to rewrite her will, leaving everything to him. When he was satisfied, he relieved her pain and set her leg. She died soon afterwards.

The household day revolved round meals and surgeries. Breakfast was served in bed at 10.00 a.m. It consisted of eggs. The previous night, a maid would arrive with a list of eggs. The choice was: one goose egg, two turkey eggs, three duck eggs, or four hen eggs. I usually chose the goose egg as it seemed less in bulk than any of the others. 'Boiled, fried, poached, scrambled or buttered?' we were asked. U.B. liked his eggs buttered, which meant melting a large lump of butter in a small bowl standing in boiling water, and whisking the eggs in the fat until they were light and frothy. They were served with fingers of toast, marmalade and coffee.

Each morning, while one maid cooked breakfast, another would go upstairs 'to prepare him'. U.B. would remain snoring until shaken by the maid, who had to pass him his false teeth, picking them out of the water-glass by the side of the bed. She then held out his dressing-gown while he heaved his bloated body from under the bedclothes, leaving his pyjama bottoms underneath the covers. He always had at least three dogs who slept on and in his bed. His bedclothes were never tucked in at the foot: they had to be left free, so that the dogs could curl under them. The sheets were always stained. In the winter, the maid would hold a large chamber-pot for U.B. to urinate into, and he would then quickly return to bed with a newly-filled stone hot-water-bottle and, propped up with numerous pillows, would settle down to his food. A.M. slept a good ten feet away from him, and would pretend to remain asleep until the 'preparation' routine was complete. Needless to say, the maids took this unpleasant task in rotation.

I was unaware of these goings-on until I was about seven years old. One night A.M. walked into my bedroom, grabbed the collar of my pyjamas and said, 'I have decided that you will now sleep with me.' I learned later that there had been a particularly vicious quarrel the evening before. U.B. had hit A.M. round the head and used most foul language. She was eventually rescued by her sister, Aunt Carrie (A.C.), who lived with them. I cannot remember how many days or weeks I had to share A.M.'s bed. It seemed an eternity, every minute of which I was afraid. A.M. used me, but at the same time she needed my support. She had no love for me – her capacity for love had been killed long ago.

Breakfast would be followed by a bath and shower. The bath was large and built with spray panels round three sides. Over it hung a powerful shower. The bath was a delight to use. It was the one part of the day that I loved. I would take a deep breath and turn on the sprays, standing in warm water with fifteen or more horizontal jets spurting from the panels at varying heights, ranging from my knees to my back. The water pressure must have been excellent. Then I rushed to the end of the bath, gasped for air, and with a twist of the wrist turned on the overhead shower and dived under the waterfall. It was wonderful – wild yet controlled, exhausting yet exhilarating. I would dearly love to have such a bath again, but I have never seen a similar one.

After breakfast, U.B. went off to one of his surgeries which was held a few miles away, and fitted in a few visits to patients before we sat down to lunch at 2.30 p.m. This was a four-course meal, followed by coffee in the drawing-room. U.B. was a repulsive eater. The rich, dark brown, mahogany dining-table would be spattered with soup, gravy and vegetables, and spilt beer or wine. He would chew the meat with his false teeth, and once the juices had been savoured and swallowed, the remaining lump of flesh would be removed by hand or spat on to the floor for the dogs to devour. He fed his dogs from fine china plates which were also used by the family. He had the first and finest cuts of meat, the dogs had the second, the aunts and I had the left-overs. I have no idea what the staff ate. After lunch came relaxation, followed by further visiting, until high tea at 6.00 p.m. when the trolley was wheeled into the drawing-room, groaning under its load. Tea was a great event – soda bread, scones, three-tiered sandwiches, yet more boiled eggs, sponge cakes, seed and fruit cakes, jams of all varieties made from the fruits of the orchard and garden. Glasses of milk were served, and tea was drunk from pretty floral china.

The late-night surgery was held at the house. It started at 11.00 p.m., and would continue until dinner which was served after midnight. This was a larger meal than lunch and dragged on interminably. Afterwards I would disappear to the dark upper regions of the house, and climb thankfully into my high double bed.

Aunt Maud's sister Carrie was a doctor's widow. She had loved her husband dearly. He died shortly after the birth of their one and only child. She came to live with her sister and brother-in-law, and spent the rest of her life in the house as the general dogsbody. It was she who tried to keep the peace between husband and wife, and was severely insulted and despised by both. She was large and fat, with black, close-cropped, straight hair. Sometimes she invited me to sleep in her bed when she thought I was particularly lonely. I would climb a chair to reach her Victorian four-poster and burrow under the thick, soft, goosedown quilt. Snug between the sheets which she had heated with the long-poled brass warming-pan filled with red-hot coals, I would watch her undressing in front of her smoking fire. When her clothes were laid over the green-velvet, high-backed chair, and her long-sleeved,

6

buttoned-up-to-the-neck nightdress was on, I would lie folded in her arms, curled in the contours of her body. This was utter bliss – heaven on earth. She would whisper stories to me until I slept, waking to another day with the memory of her body smells, her caressing hands, and the constant rise and fall of her deep breathing. She was loved by the staff and adored by me.

The Irish maids tolerated U.B.'s advances and made fun of him. When I joined them in their own quarters, I found a camaraderie and sense of fun never known by their master and mistress. In the room next to the kitchen was an old black-leaded range and round this they danced to the accordion and banjo, or sometimes a visitor's ukulele. They were always singing ballads – innumerable verses set to old Irish tunes. They had a gramophone with a horn-shaped speaker. This was brought tenderly out of a cupboard, and favourite records ranging from classical melodies to 'hit' tunes of the day crackled and grunted from its bowels. The boxes of needles were in the charge of the chauffeur, who saved money by re-sharpening them on a type of emery board. The two gardener brothers – old Pat and old Tom – who had been together throughout their lives, would sit by the grate, sucking their well-worn clay pipes, and smiling as they tapped their thick leather boots in time to the music and with husky voices joined in the choruses. They would drink steaming tea from monastic-type pudding bowls before returning to their gypsy caravan in the heart of the orchard. The back door was permanently on the latch during these carefree leisure hours, and friends came to join in the singing and dancing, though the maids often went on working while they entertained them. I remember seeing them do the ironing at a well-scrubbed wooden table, when the iron would sizzle as it was drawn over the damp starched and blued linen, radiating a unique sweet joss-stick-type smell. And watching Kate – a buxom lass – as she expertly mended the shoes. She used to crouch on the floor working over her black steel last, surrounded by sheets of leather, knives, sharpener, nails, hammer and all the paraphernalia of the cottage shoe-making industry. She would make shoes for her friends and sing loudly in time with her hammering.

The maids taught me the 'facts of life'. I would ask for an explanation of a joke or a bawdy ballad, and it would be given to me in detail, accompanied by much giggling. At one period during the Second World War, they found it amusing to watch U.B. with his women patients. The surgery was large and dark; the maids would toss a coin, and whoever won – or was it lost? – would hide in the consulting-room to watch. I became curious – why would anyone choose to be in the same room as U.B. for any length of time? 'We'll show you tonight,' the maids told me. I went with them to the surgery. There was a cupboard under the examination couch where they hid me among the cotton wool and bandages. 'There, Miss Daphne. You can look out through these round holes,' they said, laughing. 'But be quiet now, or he'll kill you, sure he will.' Before I could make a sound, the voice of U.B. was heard, and the lid of the couch was hastily closed down on top of me. The maids flicked their dusters over the medicine bottles and left me to my fate.

In my innocence I had joined in the singing of such songs as 'Roll me over, in the clover, roll me over in the clover, do it again', but the dark and dreary surgery was no bed of clover, and although the facts of life had been explained to me, and I had seen animals mating, I had no idea what the words really implied. Could I really believe my eyes as I peered through the holes in the side of the couch? Why, when certain women patients came in, was U.B. in a state of undress? What went on when they lay on the couch above my head? I thought the frame was going to break under the strain. Even more astounding – what was happening when he sat in his revolving chair with a woman sitting astride him, her legs hanging over the sides? It was an horrific sight as he grabbed at her breast, and pressed it in his mouth. With one hand he pushed the desk, and the couple whirled round and round, higher into the air until the screw locked into the spiral nut on the chair. Then they came spinning down again in the same manner, she got dressed, and he made ready for the next patient.

I lay bathed in perspiration, which became cold and tacky on my skin. I was terrified – it was a living nightmare. My hands were over my heart as I feared that someone must hear the beating of the drums inside me. As a result of that evening, I was petrified of sex in any form for many years.

As far as these women in the surgery were concerned, I can only assume that the war had deprived them of their husbands for so long that even U.B.'s attentions were a relief. Not the wildest imagination could have converted him into a lover. Many of the women were, I am sure, afraid of him. Some probably felt that in order to obtain any medical advice, they had to allow him to have 'his ways'. He would assure them that he was sterile. We were never short of food during those war years, in spite of rationing and shortages. U.B. blackmailed his patients into giving him food in lieu of payment for consultations, or perhaps as a peace offering instead of sexual satisfaction. They gave him meat, groceries and chocolates – the latter he used to eat by the pound.

What did A.M. think about his sexual escapades – for they knew no bounds? How could she close her eyes to them? When Aunt Carrie's only daughter was pregnant, she came to stay, to be near her mother during the last weeks. U.B. had booked her a room in a nursing-home nearby and announced that he would be in charge of the birth. She had to accept this because she had little money and could not afford the normal nursing-home fees. Late one night he said that he thought the child was ready to be born and told his niece to go to the surgery for an examination. She asked me to go with her, but U.B. said no, he wanted her on her own. I decided to go to bed but not long afterwards I heard a scream and rushed downstairs to find U.B. chasing his niece round the large dining-table. He was minus his trousers and she was nude. When he saw me, U.B. went back to the surgery. The tearful niece came up-stairs to my bedroom. 'I must sleep with you tonight,' she said, 'I can't be left alone.' She told me that U.B. had insisted that she should undress and lie on the surgical couch so that he could give her an ante-natal. 'I must have had my eyes closed, for I remember his heavy breathing, and I found him without his trousers climb-ing onto the couch. He held me down and tried to rape me.' As she told me her story, her labour pains started. This very nervous, highly-strung girl gave birth some hours later.

I have often wondered why U.B. waited for so many years before making any sexual advances to me. Although I was only four when I joined the household, children were not immune from his vicious attacks. Perhaps he respected my love of animals. It was the only touch of humanity in his own character. He loved, caressed and fed the dogs who roamed the house. The white billy goat (but not the black nannies) was allowed indoors (it would often share my breakfast with me in my bedroom). He kept pigs, geese, turkeys, ducks and hens.

Perhaps, too, it was because I did not answer him back, nor burst into tears. When he tried to goad me, I would withdraw into silence, pretending that I could not speak, and therefore did not retaliate. Was he the cause of the stutter I developed? It is still

9

difficult for anyone to incite me to show anger when I am hurt or angry – I become silent and try to find solace in my own company. My children maintain that this has been detrimental to them, for though they could share my joys, they thought that I was invulnerable to pain.

Aunt Maud would weep in his presence, and despise herself for doing so, for that was what he wanted. He would smile in satisfaction and triumph, and walk away, while A.M. would rush up to her bedroom and collapse on her knees in prayer, leaning on the three-cornered cane chair: this was her altar at which she sacrificed herself for his sins. There she would stay, facing the window which overlooked her beautiful garden, her lips moving rapidly in her silent prayer for patience and understanding. Sometimes she would fall asleep in this huddled position, to be woken by the dogs barking or U.B. hammering on the locked door.

Although I was not sexually assaulted by U.B. in the early years, I was certainly assaulted physically. The first time was when I was about six years old, and had been given a red bicycle – the first and last present I ever had in that house. U.B. insisted that I should ride it immediately, and within minutes I had (through fear) found my balance, and was sent hurtling down a long steep garden path. I had no idea how to stop and crashed into the house at the end of the journey. U.B. was furious: the front mudguard was buckled, and he called the chauffeur to take it to the garage for repair. I was taken by the ear, a cane was snatched from a flower-bed, and I was led upstairs to his bedroom. He started to hit me with the cane. I was too frightened to move or cry. He found a soft spot on the back of my legs and drew blood – then I saw his victorious smile. The caning stopped and the stick was placed behind one of the bedroom curtains, and I was dismissed. The bicycle was repaired and ready – for we had a very efficient garage with its own petrol pump and every conceivable mechanical tool – and I was immediately made to ride again.

On several occasions he tied the handle bars of my bicycle to the car door, made me mount, and then took the wheel, driving for several miles with me steering for dear life. I eventually fell off – fortunately falling away from the car – and I saw once again his smile of victory before I was returned to the seat of the bicycle for the journey home. After one bad fall I refused to repeat these rides and was again beaten. Wise to his new pleasure, I realised that as soon as he drew blood he was content, so I would present the weak area on the back of my legs, and soon all was over. A.M. never tried to stop these attacks, although she would often stand outside the bedroom door, waiting to pray at her chair, no doubt asking God to forgive him. Aunt Carrie was always ready to receive me. She would bathe my legs, adding TCP to the water. It stung, but I loved the smell. If A.C. was away (she frequently went to visit her married daughter), I would leave the house and grounds, and go down to the bus stop. There I would get on the first bus which came by – there were just two destinations to choose from, Manchester one way, and Liverpool the other. I rarely had any money, but as far as I remember, I was never asked for a fare. The bus conductors recognised me. Early on, one conductor had noticed the blood streaming down my leg and tried to persuade me to go to the police station, but I begged him not to take me there. I feared that if I complained, the next flogging might not end with the sight of blood.

I was thirteen when I had my final encounter with U.B. The maids believed there was trouble brewing, for he had ordered that the lock be removed from the bathroom door. 'You're not to go in there, Miss Daphne, while he's in the house,' they said. 'You must wait until he's out visiting or at his surgery.' I replied that I was safe, he had never attacked me sexually, but yes, to make them happy I would wait for my bath until he had left the house. One morning I watched the car go out of the drive. Then I went to the bathroom and turned on the taps. While the bath was filling I began to wash my teeth at the basin. I was rinsing my mouth when I happened to look in the mirror and saw him, a huge nude shape advancing towards me. The maids had taught me what to do. I felt quite calm. I waited until he was close enough, then I turned quickly round and brought my knee up hard. He fell, hitting his head on the airing-cupboard. He lay in a heap – there was no movement. I ran to my bedroom, dressed and went to the kitchen to tell the maids. One of them suggested that I should climb the old cherry tree outside the bathroom window to see if U.B. was still there. I did, and he was. He must surely be dead. Another wanted to hide me in their attic bedrooms, but I decided to use my usual escape route. I caught a bus, got off at the terminus, and walked. I must have walked for hours. Not until dinner time that night did I find myself back at the house. Did I walk back? I do not remember. Those hours are a blackness which I have never wished to penetrate.

11

I was met in the hall by A.M. 'Hurry up, you are late for dinner,' was all she said. I went into the dining-room. U.B. came in, sat down and ate a good meal. His forehead was purple and green. No one spoke. The next day I left, and although I visited A.M. again, I never stayed in the house for a night. I had had enough.

It is now over thirty years since that night. I have tried to find something kind in Uncle Bob, but apart from his devotion to his animals, I can only think of him as evil. I know of no one with whom to compare him. He and A.M. later moved to Ireland, where A.M. died. U.B. had sold all her jewellery and valuables but her fingers were so swollen with rheumatism that her wedding band and sapphire ring could not be removed. After her death in a nursing-home, U.B. went to see her laid out in the coffin. He took with him a sharp knife and amputated her finger to obtain her last possessions – no doubt to give to his mistress, who had arrived from Manchester to stay with him.

However much we accept our childhood experiences, there is no doubt that our adult attitudes are coloured by them. After my experiences with U.B., it is hardly surprising that I have grown up with a distaste for corporal punishment, and a fear of the latent sadism that may lie behind it. I have spent all my married life in a boarding-school society and I know that the subject of corporal punishment has always aroused violent emotions and arguments, both for and against.

What is the correct place of corporal punishment in school life today? What is its purpose in a school community? What are its effects, and what alternatives are available?

In part, at least, punishment is retribution. Anyone who offends against any legal system, whether in a primitive or sophisticated society, is felt to have incurred a debt. Punishment is the discharging of the debt, whether effected negatively, by physical pain, or positively, by community service. There is probably a deep psychological need, both in the victim and the offender, that this debt should be paid one way or another.

At the same time, punishment is a preventive measure. It warns the offender against breaking the rules of his society again. This too, may be achieved negatively, through fear, or positively, through education – 'teaching him the error of his ways'.

Corporal punishment can harm the boy who is punished. First and foremost, the beating may be excessive. In the brutal climate of past centuries, when physical force was seen as the only way of ensuring discipline, there were horrific instances. Stories tell of schoolboys picking bits of shirt from the backs of their friends – strips of material driven into the wounds by savage flogging. Among the first batch of students who entered Marlborough College when it opened in 1843 was Edward Lockwood. In his autobiography, *Early Days of Marlborough College*, he says:

'The knoutings which I received from my master's reverend arm, turned my back all the colours of the rainbow; and when I screamed from the fearful torture they produced, the Head Master would send a prefect down to say that if I made such a horrid noise, he also would have a go-in at me, when my master had done his worst. Occasionally two masters would be caning at the same time with the rhythm of blacksmiths hammering on an anvil. . . . When, on my arrival home, I was undressed ınd put to bed by my tender-hearted nurse, she viewed my back with the utmost horror and indignation. But she was told that as the punishment had been administered by reverend men called to the ministry, I must have deserved every blow I got.'[1]

The physical and mental damage done by that degree of punish-ment – for which there can never have been any justification in any age – is obvious enough. However, there is also the anguish of the *prospect* of punishment, particularly if it is delayed. A sensitive child may suffer acute terror beyond any reasonable retribution for a schoolboy's crime, even if the physical pain is relatively moderate. Moreover, violence breeds violence, and some boys who have suffered at the hands of masters or monitors will in turn try to cause suffering to those smaller and less adequate than themselves. Professor Terence Morris, a Criminologist in the University of London, maintains that such violence frequently remains uncontrolled in adult life.

Corporal punishment may also harm the master or monitor (where this is allowed) who administers the beating. When it affords the opportunity for latent sadism to become active, it is both degrading and harmful. Some opponents suggest that it may cause latent masochism to become overt, though this is less fully established.

Are there any good effects? One may be the establishing of dis-cipline. Established through fear, in a negative way: nevertheless, discipline and order in a school are important. Furthermore, pupils may prefer an immediate beating to a long-term punishment, provided that it is carried out according to the rules, and is accepted as consistent and fair.

An eminent Old Harrovian QC told me a lovely story recently. He was captain of the Torpids XI (under sixteen years old) of the House cricket teams, and consequently was treated with respect by housemaster and boys alike. He had returned to school at the start of one summer term with a 'girlie' magazine, mild in comparison with present-day photographs in newspapers and advertisements, but risqué by the standards of the time. After viewing the exposed bosoms, he sold it, for one shilling, to a boy in another house. Later that night the new owner was found by his own housemaster leering at – or was it ogling? – the magazine. There was an uproar. 'Where did you obtain this obscene pornography?' The new owner grassed, and his housemaster telephoned the future QC's housemaster, in outrage. 'I am taking this matter directly to the Head Master – the boy should be expelled immediately.' This was no way to win a House cricket match. The QC's housemaster cajoled, persuaded, and promised that if his fellow-master would leave the matter to him, he would 'beat the living daylights' out of the offender.

'I didn't think it odd to be summoned out of bed at such a late hour,' the QC told me. 'It wasn't unusual for my housemaster to discuss tactics at any hour of the day when there was a cricket match to be won.' He went to the study dressed in his pyjamas and found a black-visaged and fuming master who asked, 'Have you seen this before?' pointing to the literature on his desk. 'I admitted my guilt immediately and was told what the consequences could have been. I was extremely grateful to think that no more would be said after what would prove a painful few minutes. The Head of House was summoned and we went into the large drawing-room – where a sofa was cleared – and I had six of the very best. It is at times such as this that corporal punishment has a place in the discipline of the school. The housemaster, who was considered by many to be an old buffer, had acted immediately once his decision had been made, and all three parties were satisfied. After the ordeal, I thanked my executioner for his understanding.' The boy eventually became Head of School.

A similar story concerns a Lord Chancellor and a managing director of a publishing firm who had been contemporaries at a well-known school. At the early age of fourteen, the future Lord Chancellor returned to his Alma Mater with the most pornographic magazine he could lay his hands on in those days – *La Vie Parisienne*. Having read it avidly from cover to cover, he left it for his friend's enjoyment inside a tuck-box. An energetic house-master, making his rounds that evening, found this obscene publication and immediately called the future publisher to his study. To the boy's amazement, his housemaster announced that the matter was too serious for him to deal with, and that he had asked the Head Master to cope with the situation. The Head Master (later to become Dean of a University renowned for its Theological School) settled down in a comfortable chair, and placed the magazine on the table between the boy and himself. For the next half hour, master and pupil worked their way through the pages. The boy was given a full biological lesson on the structure of a woman's body in relation to its function, with particular reference to sexual enjoyment. The lesson completed, the boy was given six of the best before returning to his bed. This story has a postscript. Years later the publisher was sent the manuscript of a book of poems. 'They were atrocious, and in no way could I have published them. The author came to collect his rejected manuscript, and to my surprise, I found myself face to face with my old Head Master. He accepted defeat graciously, and as we parted he looked knowingly at me. I swear it was with some hint of recognition,' said the former pupil.

Corporal punishment is not the only means of venting sadism. Like U.B., a sadist will use whatever means are available. Holding a boy up to ridicule before the class is one such method, and in some ways this is worse. A boy who can withstand a beating may rightly feel that he has won the encounter, while open ridicule leaves him bewildered and unable to retaliate. When my eldest daughter was about eleven, her Geography mistress consistently ridiculed her before the class. On one occasion, my husband and I combined to write her Geography essay with the help of the Head of the Geography Department at the school where John was Head Master. When Siobhan handed it in, the mistress said, without reading it: 'And this is what I think of Siobhan's homework'; then tore it up in front of the pupils. With this sort of treatment, any child will quickly refuse to work at all.

In the past, when physical brutality was commonplace, perhaps it is true to say that there was no alternative to beating; but there are certainly alternatives today, and many of them, from learning by heart passages of the Bible, Shakespeare, or T. S. Eliot (and I do

15

not believe that this deters students from reading good English in the future – it may even encourage them), or washing the head-master's car, to the final public-school sanctions of rustication and expulsion. These last are a headmaster's ultimate weapons, and very potent ones. Their effect is twofold: the immediate loss of face, and the future damage to career prospects. Given the range of alternatives, I believe there is no longer any need for corporal punishment in a public school. Just as violence breeds violence, so lack of violence between master and pupil will result in a diminution of bullying among the pupils themselves. But there must be rules in any society, and they must be accepted and obeyed. It takes a positive attitude on the part of housemasters, assistant masters and monitors, to make a school disciplined and successful. A school is only as good as its staff. I once knew a head-master who insisted that the private lives of his staff were their own concern, and nothing to do with the school. He was wrong. Masters inevitably bring their attitudes and ways of thought into their teaching, and these – rather than the actual words spoken – are what is learnt.

I have spoken, so far, of public schools. The problems which face the headmaster of a state school are rather different. He is obliged by law to provide an education up to the school-leaving age of sixteen, and therefore cannot expel. Moreover, most state schools are too new to have built up much in the way of tradition and self-government, so that the whole tone of the school depends on the headmaster. It is possible, therefore, that he should continue to be allowed to use corporal punishment as his final deterrent. Both the teaching profession and the parents are sufficiently aware of the dangers for the control to be adequate – the danger could be of excessive control and insufficient freedom of action for the headmaster.

Although I have no experience of teaching in a state school, I do sit as a magistrate. Confronted with reports on young offenders who frequently play truant from school, only turning up on days when there is anything interesting in the programme, I see something of the enormity of the problem facing state-school head-masters. Boys and girls have told me that they 'sign-in' daily, and promptly leave by the back door, and that the teachers are well aware of it, turning a blind eye to keep the educational authorities at bay.

2

Schooldays

Aunt Maud believed in using corporal punishment on me, particularly when I was being forgetful or untidy (she abhorred chaos, although she lived in a state of constant muddle). She had a deft hand with the Mason Pearson hairbrush, but would never touch the cane used by Uncle Bob which he kept behind the curtain of one of the windows in his bedroom. Once A.M. realised where it was hidden, she refused to draw that curtain at night. It was as though she blamed the cane for being evil, encouraging U.B. in his sadistic pleasures. Uncle Bob enjoyed inflicting pain.

Unlike most children I would count the days until I could return to school, for I was fortunate that none of my schools practised this form of discipline. In my 'teens I often spent the holidays visiting friends. I stayed with a large number of families, and found that homes could be run and discipline maintained without resorting to constant physical violence. I was never beaten by anyone other than my guardians.

My first school was a pre-preparatory boarding-school in the heart of Cheshire, where children stayed until the age of eight. When I went there England was on the verge of the Second World War. There were only two other boarders and we shared the same dormitory.

My companions were a girl and boy, both two years my senior. We had a kind and young matron, whom we called 'Nanny'. I think she must have made a habit of opening the door to our room late at night to see that all was well before going to bed herself. If

17

she found that I was awake – which I invariably was – she would stay beside me and gently stroke my forehead, running her fingers through my hair; softly sing the Lord's Prayer, and follow this with old songs of gnomes and princesses, of knights and giants. She never discussed things or asked me questions. I was happy to have the undivided attention of this beautiful person at this late hour. She relaxed me, caressed me and lulled me to peaceful sleep. I do not know her name, nor have any idea from which part of the country she came, but I would like her to know that it was she who made my first encounter with boarding-school bearable. I never saw her during the day.

The other boy and girl were in the same form, and each tried to outdo the other in bravery. The boy won when one day he brought a lot of worms and placed them on the girl's bed.

'Eat them,' he said to her, and she visibly shrank away.

The worms crawled over the sheet, leaving a shiny slime in their path.

'Eat them, you coward,' he cried.

'Eat them yourself,' was her reply.

He tossed back his blankets to reveal the worms in his bed. He carefully got in beside them, lay on his back, and holding up a worm, slowly manipulated the wriggling creature into his mouth, and swallowed it.

I was promptly sick.

For weeks afterwards, this boy continued to make a meal of worms on going to bed. I cannot remember whether the girl was brave enough to devour them, but she used to collect spiders and cockroaches together with a few worms, and sleep with them as her companions. I would remain silent, and long for them to doze off, so that Nanny could come.

I am sure that it was the physical contact with Nanny which I needed more than anything – for love flows through contact. Too often we are afraid to touch each other. Even within families there is embarrassment. Recently I was at a crowded committee meeting. A middle-aged man, a friend of mine, walked in and said: 'What a foul day! I woke up this morning and cuddled my wife – I wish I were still cuddling her.' There was a sudden silence, and he continued, 'We're a cuddling family – we cuddle our children, even though the youngest is at university, and they cuddle us back. We love being together.' There was a sense of shock in the room, but no one could deny that this man was always happy and contented, and that his wife and he have a very special affinity.

My days in this first school were lonely. I was afraid of making friends with the other children who went home each night. I could not understand their conversations about their families, whom I had never met, and they tended to stick together and spend their out-of-school hours visiting each other's houses.

I became obsessed by one of the maids who used to lay the dining-tables. She had a permanent drip at the end of her long, thin and pointed nose. We had a piece of bread or a roll at lunch time, and I would stand behind the curtain to see where the drips would land, and then I would know where to sit for the meal. Breakfast for the three of us was more difficult, as she would serve out the cereal or porridge, so I always offered to 'wait' and collect the dishes from her in order to have a drip-free cereal. Rather unkind of me – but perhaps it did not matter so much to two children accustomed to a diet of worms.

The school was situated between Manchester and Liverpool. War was declared in September 1939, and soon the sirens sounded nightly to announce the presence of German bombers, raiding the great cities of Merseyside. There was an 'air-raid table' under which we were meant to sleep during these raids, but it was so flimsy that no one ever bothered to put us there. Our blue 'siren-suits' were used as dressing-gowns, and gas masks were kept under our beds. My identity disc hung round my neck day and night with my number, LFHH 41-6, to give me a name, dead or alive.

At the age of seven I left this school and was sent to board with a family in Lincolnshire. I found myself among a mass of girls in a highly efficient establishment. I was happy there, but unhappy in the family. After one term, I was transferred back to Cheshire, and spent a term at the High School before being sent to the Lake District.

The next school was at Windermere, and was owned by a large and homely headmistress. She did not teach, but on Sundays we all gathered in the beautiful old Victorian drawing-room and she read us stories. Furniture filled every nook and cranny. Spanish shawls were draped over the grand piano, lace mats and cushions were used with gay abandon, and china figures, photographs and vases of flowers covered all available surfaces. Old-rose velvet curtains hung at the windows and strange faces from bygone ages peered down from the walls, dusty and dark from the smoke of the open fires – the drying oil paint cracking their features. Her smell pervaded the room, which she never left. It gave me a sense of total security to know that she was always there. Her lack of exercise made her very large, and when she sat down in her special chair, she had to heave up her bosom and place it on her knee. Her hair was tied in a wild bun on the back of her head, yet her Victorian clothes gave her dignity. She sometimes remembered my name, but more often than not referred to me as 'You there'.

She had a dragon of a secretary who domineered over us all. Although I was used to corporal punishment from Uncle Bob, I did strongly object when my knuckles were whipped with her ruler for no other reason than to draw attention to herself. She was thin and bitter, but devoted to the Head.

I remember the Art classes at this school. The Art master eventually had to admit that I was a hopeless student, and in desperation made me sit on the platform, gave me books by Rider Haggard to read, and told me to sit still. He started sketching my portrait, and became so involved that I spent all future Art classes engrossed in my reading. He said he was going to show my picture at the Royal Academy. Years later I learnt that the Royal College of Art had been evacuated to Windermere, and I imagine that he was a College lecturer.

It was a happy school – I can recall only one instance of a girl's running away. Left to learn to get on with each other, we were given a considerable amount of freedom. It was good for us. We had an innocent time with midnight walks up the mountains, or night-riding bareback on the ponies in the neighbouring field. Out of the group of girls I remember two in particular. One was an old-fashioned girl who returned after a half-term exeat in a state of great distress. She had been told that she was an adopted child, and broke down with the shock of the news. Two spinster sisters had adopted her, and she had never thought it strange to be without a father. Perhaps she was the illegitimate child of one of them. If so, I think she would have preferred to know it, as she kept saying: 'I wasn't wanted.' I envied her, for she was greatly loved and wanted now. The other was a girl who went walking on the hills with her sister during the holidays. On returning home they were given a bowl of hot water to wash their feet. Her sister leant over to a lamp to turn it on and was immediately electrocuted. The parents decided at once to have another child in memory of her. A daughter was born to whom they gave the same name as the deceased child. They hoped for a child identical with the one they had lost.

In the summer of 1946 I reached the top of the school, and it was time to move on. I spent a brief period, about a week, at another school, where I was wrongly accused of stealing a hairbrush. The Head Mistress picked on me as the culprit. Perhaps she thought that as I was the only child without a family, I was an easy target for retribution. I ran away to Duns in Berwickshire, where I had spent part of the previous school holidays. The family with whom I had stayed were not pleased to see me. I was packed back to my official guardian in Cheshire, Uncle Bob, beaten as usual, and the next day was taken to Manchester Station. He had tied a luggage label round my neck which I was unable to read: I had no idea where I was going. In silence U.B. and A.M. walked up the platform to the guard; I was handed over to him, and he was instructed to chain me in the mail van. They stood and supervised him. Not a word was spoken to me. As soon as the train left the station, this good man immediately unchained me. I am sure that there were tears in his eyes.

'God forgive me for obeying them,' he said, 'God forgive me. They said to treat you as a dog, and not to speak to you.'

'Where are we going?' I asked.

'You don't know?' – and he cut the label from around my neck and read it. 'Perth, Scotland, and we won't get there till nearly midnight.'

My father had been Scottish. Was that why this school had been chosen? Or was it merely because it could take me at short notice?

Midnight found me on Perth Station. A small wiry woman ran up to me – 'Are you Daphne?'

'Yes,' I replied, 'I'm Daphne.'

'Good, I am Miss Ross, your Head Mistress – come along, the car is waiting.'

We had a hair-raising journey with Miss Ross at the wheel. There was a howling gale, and the rain beat down on the windows. I glimpsed the solemn faces of Highland cattle in the headlights, before we swept into a long driveway and arrived at a very grand entrance.

'We had to be evacuated from Edinburgh to here,' said Miss Ross, 'I can't think why as there are no bombs. We had a fire the other day,' she added, 'but only part of the building is damaged. I fear the roof leaks where you are sleeping, but I've got a selection of wellingtons for you to try on – you'll need them to get to your bed.'

It was an icy building built of stone. Many of the floors were unadorned stone – only in the grand reception rooms and main bedrooms did matured wood shine under our feet. During the winter months, with the girls crowding the passages, the walls would perspire, and a steady stream of water would run along the flagstones. After a night of heavy frost – and there were many – the water in the passages froze. I awoke to find that the moisture from my breath had frozen on the sheets. When I had plucked up enough courage, I would jump out of bed, the ice crackling as I pushed the sheet away from me. My flannel – hard and stiff – would have to be prised off the marble slab. My friends and I slid at speed down the passage to the bathroom.

There was gas lighting, giving a softer glow than today's electricity, but it was bad for our eyes. Apart from myself and one other girl, who both managed to sit beside lights, all the girls in my form had to wear glasses. We did have electricity which originated from a temperamental engine. This vast piece of mechanical ingenuity sat in state in the back courtyard. It groaned in its labour, and its ancient parts creaked, rheumatic through lack of oil, in order to bring to birth a feeble glimmer of light. The energy source was the river Tay which flowed through the grounds, but no matter whether the river was in full flood or low with summer heat, the engine would work only when it wished to.

Out in the courtyard there was also an ancient pump, though the school was attached to the mains water supply. I volunteered to pump all drinking water for the meals. It was pure and beautiful, sweet from the hills, but rarely appreciated by anyone except me. I was considered odd to use up my energy pumping when all one had to do was turn on the tap.

There were deer and Highland cattle in the grounds. In the spring the cattle became ferocious guarding their young. On Sundays, when we had to walk to church by way of a drive where the cattle roamed freely, we would pray that the Good God would protect us! Meat was still rationed in these post-War years, but we were always well supplied. The venison must surely have come from our vast estate.

My need for solitude would sometimes overcome my dislike of cold, and there were occasions, even in winter, when I would retreat to one of the toilets on the top floor just to be alone. The mahogany toilets sat on platform 'thrones'. Large brass handles operated the flush, revealing blue-and-white Scottish castles painted on the china bowls. I sat and read the hours away.

There was a better place, however – a forbidden garden which was wild and wonderful. Magnificent trees brought from all over the world flourished here. I would climb on top of the overgrown rhododendron bushes and use them as a footpath, or sit there and read on my own. It was a jungle-type vegetation, the branches reaching out for light and quite uncontrolled. Under the same rhododendrons, I walked amongst the trunks whilst pitch black above me were the flowering shrubs. It was here, underneath, that the deer remained undisturbed and free. I rarely heard of any of my contemporaries using this place. I was alone with Nature. Although the garden was forbidden us, I felt no sense of wrong in being in such a place – where the early flowers of spring bloomed in their splendid array of yellows and blues, followed by the wild roses and strawberries, the rare orchids and exotic toadstools – where the deer ran with the rabbits and hares, and night-time was safe for the badgers and moles. I spent hours in wonder under the trees from the East and from the Americas which had been lovingly planted a century ago. Sometimes I would burst into song, and run with the deer sharing their freedom, or turn cart-wheels and dance. It was here that God gave me an understanding and knowledge of Himself in His beauty, and with open arms I would say 'Thank you'. I love company, and happiness, and laughter, but all my life I have needed solitude to be at peace with myself, to be aware of Nature and to be part of that infinity which is another name for God.

Throughout my years at this school, we hardly came into contact with the staff outside the form-room. I do not recall our having 'pashes' on mistresses, but there were certainly many relationships between girls themselves. Younger girls would become obsessed with an older girl, and consequently everything was done for her – her bed was made, her shoes cleaned, dishes washed, and innumerable sweets left under the pillow (a great sacrifice as sweets were still on ration). It was not unnatural, it was a way of expressing love.

Miss Ross trusted us all and we did our best to live up to her expectations. She was an eccentric and delightful person. Although she did not teach, she knew us all. On Wednesdays she would drive into Perth to early Communion and I would join her. She was a dangerous and chaotic driver. She skidded along the roads, scraping the side of the bridge over the Tay, and being stopped by the police for speeding, faulty tyres, and travelling in the dark without lights. 'You'll kill yourself one of these days,' she was told – and she did. I missed her.

Headship is a powerful position – a very lonely place to be. A bad Head can destroy the fibre of staff and pupils alike. Miss Ross's successor was a strict disciplinarian and she hated youth, or was envious of it. In the three terms I had with her, I understood all the damage a Head could cause to pupils. I re-member a particularly unhappy incident. I had kept out of the way of this new Head Mistress, and she was suspicious because I did so. One day we were summoned into her drawing-room for a lesson on sex education. I was not particularly interested, and at the end of the talk, when we were invited to submit questions to the visiting speaker, I did not contribute. The Head Mistress watched me and in a loud voice said, 'Daphne is the only one who knows about this subject already. She does not need further enlighten-ment,' she added sarcastically.

The major problems of boarding-school life, now as then, are jealousy and bullying. Jealousy is inevitable in closed communi-ties, from schools to monasteries – even though it may go un-recognised as the root cause of problems encountered there. I was once sadly disillusioned while sitting on a school's Govern-ing Body Committee. I wanted the Governors to meet the pupils and staff. The Committee was not enthusiastic, and the Head Master was downright hostile. I felt that we were governing the school from a sort of limbo. A fellow member, a bishop, saw my distress, and asked me to join him at his beautiful home in the Cathedral Close. I was soon relaxed in front of a log fire. For tea there was a choice of raspberry, gooseberry, black- and red-currant jams to accompany fresh scones still warm from the Aga cooker. Fishing-rods were standing by the french windows, and mine host, the Bishop, was proud to supply the family dinner once a week with freshly-caught trout from his own stream. His wife had made their home truly homely. Chintz curtains and chair covers blended well with the walls and carpets. The last of the summer roses radiated peace from the shining silver rose bowls whose reflected beauty glowed deep in the mahogany furniture. It was late afternoon, and the sun cast its mellow rays in farewell before sinking behind the cedars at the end of the garden. I was unwound and happy – my school committee meeting was an age away – there was stillness and tranquillity.

I was rudely awakened when I remembered that I had to return to London, and that there was a train to catch. It was hard to tear myself away from such idyllic surroundings and such amiable hosts. As I left I remarked: 'Surely you can never know the true difficulties of life – you live in a beautiful house, in a beautiful county, and in what must be one of the most beautiful cathedral closes in Britain. It must be impossible to remember the realities of life.'

'No,' came the surprising reply, 'there is more hypocrisy and jealousy in a cathedral close than you can find anywhere else in the country.'

I stared in amazement, and turned to his wife – 'Yes, Daphne, that is so – but perhaps it is the same in any closed community.'

The Bishop and his wife were wise and right. For the past twenty-five years I have lived as a master's wife in a series of boarding-schools which admitted only boys (the last of these is Westminster, now gallantly allowing girls to take advantage of the excellent sixth-form teaching, and having the added advantage of being situated in central London). I have no experience of living in a co-educational adolescent community with a well-mixed teaching staff, but I do believe that some at least of the problems are confined to schools which are predominantly single-sex.

Jealousy among the youngest boys starts very early. Preparatory schools may be the breeding-ground. A boy of any age, introduced to a ready-made community, is confronted with two courses of action. The first is to make a name for himself in whatever field he feels that he can excel – in sport or academic work, in music or art, in acting or stage management, in being on good terms with the masters or becoming the school's comic and teller of Irish jokes. The alternative is for the boy to fade into the background, and get on with his work and play without making himself conspicuous in any way. This may lead to few friends and can lay him open to a type of bullying. Some boys may admire his bravery as he ignores popularity, but it will take time for the loner to be accepted.

I remember a dreadful period when I was nine years old, and attending a well-established day school. Younger than most at the school, I was not prepared to fight for popularity, and I jealously

25

guarded my freedom from those pressures when I found myself, yet again, in a new world: a world apart from the adults, going from a society which I abhorred – the misery of life at U.B.'s – to one which I disliked the thought of entering. So I became a recluse, and found myself being an easy prey for others. It soon become clear that others could attack me and I would not retaliate. Girls vied with each other to see if they could break me.

Sports Day was a great event. Parents arrived early, and took the girls out to lunch or to a picnic in the grounds. The form leader, a particular bully of mine, laughed aloud for all to hear: 'Daphne has no parents – we don't ask where she came from – were you really found under a gooseberry bush? By the Devil, I suppose!' She was our great athlete, and the fiercest fighter in the mock battles. My emotions got the better of me and I wept.

The first race in the afternoon was the hurdles – which I won. The second event was the long jump – which I won. The races progressed, and I carefully entered for the ones that I knew I could win, until finally came the *pièce de résistance*, the hundred yards sprint, my favourite, and hers – and I won.

The rest of the form had looked aghast at each victory, and the next day I was confronted by a group whose leader, yesterday's rival, threatened to 'do me in'. Jealousy knew no bounds. At Break I was led outside. My aggressor was waiting to fight. Her leadership was in jeopardy, and had to be maintained at all costs. Yes, I had put her into second place in all the events of the previous day – but she was still a good deal taller than I, and anyway I was unlikely to retaliate – 'she hasn't got the guts'. A large group of girls joined hands and formed a circle round us, shouting gibes. I was locked inside this human wall, and stood horrified as the girls' laughter gave way to snarls and accusations of cowardice. I was a fighting cock which would not fight. My opponent would spring forward with a quick thrust of her fist to my head or body, and away again, laughing. I felt claustrophic as the chanting taunts grew louder. Suddenly my rage got the better of me, and I attacked. My oppressor was not prepared for my instantaneous change of behaviour, and found herself bruised, cut and lying immobile on the grass. The silence was overwhelming.

I was not terrorised again, and instead girls vied for my friendship – but I was not interested. I had learnt the meaning of hypocrisy at a much earlier age, and I was sick with contempt. I wanted to be left alone.

26

When I sat an exam to pass into the middle school, I spent a delightful time ensuring that my answers would result in my justifiably leaving this school altogether.

I write this episode of my life, not because I am either proud or ashamed of it, but because I know what it is to experience both the physical and mental horrors of being tormented by adults and by children of my own age.

The old stories of bullying can still be paralleled today, though there is perhaps less general cruelty. In the eighteen-thirties, before the growth in popularity of organised sports, the most popular entertainment at Harrow was 'toozling' – chasing and killing birds in the school hedgerows. Many of the boys kept a dog and cats – the one to kill the others. They were expert stone-throwers: it is said that no dog could live on Harrow Hill, and frequently ponies pulling carts past the school were blinded.

Other schools were no better. In his autobiography, *Paint and Prejudice*, C. R. Nevinson describes his experiences at Uppingham in about 1905:

'As a result of my sojourn in this establishment for the training of sportsmen I possessed at the age of fifteen a more extensive knowledge of "sexual manifestations" than many a "gentleman of the centre". It is possible that the masters did not know what was going on . . . It is now the fashion to exclude "the hearties" from accusations of sexual interest or sadism, or masochism; but in my day it was they, the athletes, and above all the cricketers, who were allowed these traditional privileges. Boys were bullied, coerced and tortured for their diversion, and many a lad was started on strange things through no fault nor inclination of his own.

Games and the practice of games were the order of the day . . . I was a good runner, and I seldom was whipped by the hunting-crops of the "hearties", who would ride beside us lashing out at any fellow with stitch or cramp. I was also able to follow the hounds on foot in the great hunting county and thereby escape many a flogging.

I think it was the kicking which finally settled matters. In this popular pastime known as the "flying kick" the cricket eleven wore their white shoes and any junior was captured and bent over for their sport. They took running kicks at our posteriors, their white shoes marking the score and a certain place counting as a bull. A period of this marksmanship left me inflamed and constipated, and eventually I developed acute appendicitis, an illness much dreaded in those days, as the operation was thought to be extremely dangerous. Thank God, I became so ill that I was moved to London . . . I was in a wretched state, septic in mind and body.'[2]

Young boys are no longer held over open fires to burn the pants off them, but only last month I heard of a boy going to his first boarding-school where he had his head thrust down the lavatory and the chain pulled. Another boy left the same school black and blue, with bruises over his face and body, and would not say how they were received; and a third boy, aged fifteen, who declined to participate in the latest vogue of glue-sniffing combined with smoking and drinking, in retaliation was stripped, day after day, thrust under the shower and left naked. He refused to return to school after an exeat.

A friend told me how, some years ago, when he was at preparatory school, his form decided to 'take the mickey' out of a quiet new boy. They roped him to a chair and said they would slowly cut his throat with a razor. They told him to say his last prayer. One boy who had previously cut his finger-nail into a sharp point proceeded to imitate the razor, while his friends held the struggling new boy in his execution chair. The struggle unexpectedly stopped – they thought he was fooling them, and joining in their sadistic games. When the melée was over, his head was released and it flopped to one side. 'He's a good sport,' said one with trepidation. The ropes were loosened, and the body fell to the floor. 'Died of shock' was the verdict – a victim of bullying.

Unnatural death is not perhaps as uncommon among school children and students as some people may think. In America suicide is the third highest cause of death in the eighteen-to-twenty-one age group. 'The child had a disturbed mind' – but had he, and what disturbed him? How much bullying does go on in any school? Mental bullying is as disastrous as physical.

Jealousy is nearly always at the root of the problem. It is the one apart who suffers – to be a loner in early life is to invite the persecutor, and to be an easy prey. He will learn the meaning of victimisation and continual harassment. He may in turn become the aggressor, picking on younger boys, or carrying his aggression into married life, where there is only one to persecute; or, because he knows what it is to walk in constant fear and loneliness, he may be given the grace to reach the depths of love and compassion. I do not maintain that it is necessary to suffer in order to have compassion, only to say that as the result of great unhappiness a child can either be psychologically disturbed for life, or be prepared to alleviate suffering in others by not accepting hypocrisy or bullying in any form. Fear and terror may be the seeds of tolerance. Despair may lead to hope.

Neither do I maintain that bullying to such a degree is commonplace. Severe bullying may depend on one or two boys only, boys who have experienced the taste of power and then pick on some unfortunate member of their year to be the victim. Hence it is not everyone on an 'intake' who has to suffer, nor does one form – or House – necessarily influence the next.

My daughter Penelope was an attractive child – she was good at games, and had a quiet personality. We sent her to a day school where most of the girls came from wealthy homes. They knew that her father was headmaster of a boys' boarding-school. Was it her looks which were the initial invitation to an attack of mental bullying, or was it the fact that she was living in a young and enviable male society? Perhaps it was both. Penelope was asked by the girls at her school to arrange parties at home – this she refused to do. She was asked to arrange introductions, and again she refused, for she knew her father would disapprove. She was ostracised by her fellow students within a few days of arriving at her new school. It was not long before they realised that her financial situation was nowhere near as satisfactory as theirs, and she was ah easy victim of mental cruelty. One day, during a rainy Break, she heard the girls discussing shampoos. They all seemed to pay a weekly visit to a well-known hairdresser, and each girl had her individual shampoo. She had never heard of so many brand names – mostly in French! Penelope's hair is beautiful. At last a girl turned to her and said:

'Which hairdresser do you go to, Penelope? Does he use a particular shampoo for you?'

'My mother is my hairdresser,' she replied quietly, 'and she uses Boots' Family Shampoo for us all.'

There was a stunned silence, then a girl laughed and said, 'We use that for our dogs.'

Children – no matter how young – must be made aware of the consequences of bullying, either mental or physical. It is not difficult to explain the horrors, and to ask your child to stand up for others and protect the victimised. Very often a few moments of courage on behalf of a young child may curtail untold misery.

A dull, plain boy, or a boy who is going through the difficult adolescent age when acne is acute and dandruff an embarrassment, suffers another type of jealousy. Whom does this boy wish to emulate? Obviously the one whom he most admires in looks or valour. He wants to be associated with this 'friend' (as he wishes him to be) and is jealous of all others who have claims. He becomes possessive and tries hard to impress. He desperately needs to be recognised and appreciated. It is not difficult to imagine the various ways and means of being noticed. It is of course easier if you have money. Money can buy gifts, favours and admiration.

I was staying on the Continent with the parents of a Harrow boy when they were disturbed by a telephone call from him:

'Please would you make sure, Mother, that you hire a Rolls Royce, nothing else, for Speech Day. And it would be a good idea to purchase a picnic box from Fortnum & Mason's – "champers" of course. I want you to meet a friend of mine – he may be able to join us during the day.'

The parents were wealthy, but they did not flaunt their wealth. Their immediate reaction was that their son must be homosexually inclined. I do not think they were correct. Homosexuality was, and is, so feared that ordinary problems of relationships are often ignored. Their son was small, spotty and greasy-haired. His 'friend' was tall, clear-skinned and popular, and as his parents lived on the other side of the globe, they would not be at Speech Day. The son wanted the Rolls Royce to impress, and he was anxious in case his 'friend' spent the day in another's company. He knew that it went against the grain for his parents to indulge in such ostentation. Nevertheless, he asked them, and they decided to comply with his wishes.

It is not unknown for boys wanting to impress their fellow students to dictate to their family the smallest detail of the exact mode of clothing to be worn, and which jewellery should be donned by the ladies. This may in part be due to embarrassment, but it is frequently connected with rivalry, competitiveness and possessiveness, all of which may be associated with jealousy. As a boy at Harrow, Byron wrote on July 2, 1805, to his beloved half-sister, Augusta, persuading her to visit the school to hear him give a passionate speech from King Lear's address to the storm:

'I *beg Madam* you may make your appearance in one of his Lordships most *dashing* carriages, as our Harrow *etiquette* admits of nothing but the most *superb* vehicles, on our Grand *Festivals*.'[3]

He may have wished to impress a fellow pupil, Charles David

Gordon, who was some years younger than himself. Byron called Gordon his 'dearest Friend', and wrote urging him to pay a visit to his country seat, Newstead Abbey:

'No one ever will be a more welcome Guest than yourself. Nor is there any one whose correspondence can give me more pleasure, or whose friendship yield me greater delight than yours.'[3]

Eccentricity in parents is normally accepted and may even be encouraged. I was happy to find that my own children never told us what to wear or how to behave at the various school functions, but when I discussed this with my eldest daughter, rather pleased that my beloved offspring had such confidence in us, she promptly disillusioned me. 'Mother, you're both rather odd – a law unto yourselves. If we made comments, you might do something beyond the limit – but now that you mention it, yes we *do* have a request. Please don't wear your half-moon reading-glasses on a chain round your neck.' I made one attempt to conform to their wishes, lost my glasses in my usual haphazard way, and found that the only way I could preserve my sanity was to chain them to me. The children were kind, and the subject was not mentioned again except in a frivolous manner.

Jealousy may have a rather different effect on an older boy who finds himself pursued and admired by younger boys. His privacy has vanished – wherever he turns, there is someone nearby posses- sively happy in his presence. The role has compensations: his boots will be polished for him, his bed made, and his tastes satis- fied, whether for cream cakes or cigarettes. A boy has to be mature enough to cope with the situation, knowing how much he can accept, when and how to say no, when to be on friendly terms, and when to remain aloof. He may be laying a foundation for his future behaviour in adult life. Suppose he is good-looking, aca- demically brilliant, excellent at sport? He will probably carry these qualities into adulthood – marry a good-looking woman with a zest for life – reach the heights of his profession. Happiness in family and work, ability and achievement, good health, a sense of humour and good countenance, all will inevitably cause resent- ment and bitterness in those envious of him, even though these feelings may be suppressed. All along the line, the more successful he is, the more he will be aware of jealousy.

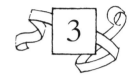

Holidays

I was fortunate in my friends at school – I never lacked for holiday invitations although I came perilously near the end of some terms without one. I was far too proud to drop a hint, especially in the later years. Instead I would wander round the fields and woods and soon forget my despondent mood as I watched the antics of the animals and birds surrounding me. My one dread was that I would have to knock on the Head Mistress's door and ask permission to stay at the school – not that I minded being on my own, in a way I think I would have welcomed the situation, but I dreaded the upheaval I might have caused, or being advised to go to an organised holiday home.

I remember my first term at Windermere. I had made friends with a girl who suffered from severe attacks of asthma. I shared her bedroom as she wanted a companion and I was happy to leave an over-excited dormitory. We had made all sorts of plans for the week's break at half-term, but a few days before the event Jane was taken home, gasping for breath and with a high temperature. I heard nothing from the family and presumed that they had forgotten the arrangements which had been made. I watched the cars rolling up the driveway, delighted girls greeting their parents, and then disappearing out of sight. I planned my escape at the end of the morning: I would slip away to the empty Sanatorium (a Swedish-type wooden building, surrounded by trees, which stood in the school grounds) without the staff's knowing I was there, and would reappear when the other girls were due to return to school.

As I was making my escape, surreptitiously carrying my wellingtons and a small suitcase, a uniformed chauffeur stepped out of a large, magnificent, white Bentley sports car, with an open roof, and special trunks fitted at the rear. 'Excuse me, Miss. I am looking for Miss Jane Darlington's friend, Miss Daphne, I'm to take her to Melling Hall.' I dropped my case and the wellingtons rolled under the car. 'I'm Jane's friend Daphne,' I said, restraining myself from throwing my arms round his neck. Quickly regaining my dignity I continued, 'I was expecting you.'

I still savour that journey. I sat in the front of the car, over the moon with joy and pride.

When I arrived at Melling Hall, I was taken to the day nursery where Jane was being entertained by Nanny. It was a well-organised household, Jane being the youngest of a family of nine. A great event had just taken place as one of her sisters was in the private maternity wing of the house, and had been delivered that day of a daughter. The midwife brought in the child to show us – never had I seen such a tiny babe. She took the infant to the window and said, 'Look at her eyes.' They were pink. The child was albino and grew up to be strikingly lovely. This was my first introduction to the Darlington family: after my visit I had an open invitation to return whenever I wanted to stay there. I used to pray that the Darlingtons would adopt me, but it never crossed their minds, and I was too shy to broach the subject.

Melling was a beautiful house. There seemed to be so many rooms: ballroom, billiard room, studies, two dining-rooms, various hallways and a large veranda; the servants' quarters were unending, and two large Agas were in constant use for baking – but we rarely penetrated this area except on Sundays when the staff were free. On that day we would go to the village church, where the family had its own separate pews, and then drive to a Lancaster hotel which still retained a gracious old Victorian aura: long halls and lounges with high ceilings and sparkling chandeliers, elderly soft-footed waiters in immaculate black uniform dexterously carrying their silver trays and attending to the comfort of guests.

Jane and I must have looked an odd sight. Her parents were dressed in well-worn typical country tweeds, but as the war was on, and we had to be economical with clothing coupons, Jane and I followed at the rear in borrowed tweed coats, so long that the sleeves reached down to our knees, and black, clodhopping, laced shoes, which had been used by her brothers. We were disrobed by smiling maids with white frilled aprons and caps, only to reveal thick, long, hairy skirts over brown woollen stockings and, if we were fortunate, multi-coloured jumpers made from odd balls of wool unravelled from worn-out woollens and knitted up again. We did not mind appearing in such eccentric clothes, which were accepted as a means of helping the war effort. It was important to give employment to the elderly and the unfit, to grow our own food in the grounds, to fish the rivers; and outgrown or discarded clothing was carefully sorted, repaired, recycled, and sent in large bundles to soldiers 'at the Front'.

Part of Melling was turned into an emergency hospital. Old sheets were torn up for bandages, and local villagers volunteered to help nurse, cook or clean. Lady Darlington (whom I called Aunt Daisy) had been a VAD nurse in the First World War and enthusiastically took charge of the administration. Many years after the war was over, she was still making beds and washing patients at the local hospital, and helping at nursing-homes so that nurses could attend church services. She was a person who cared for others. Constantly visiting the sick and the elderly, she still made time for her family. Even when she rested, she would sit in an armless high-backed chair so that her elbows were free for her to knit. How many miles of garments came from her needles? Until the end of her life (she died in 1980) she would cycle to visit the elderly and change their library books for them, and was amused to learn that she was the eldest resident in the village.

Uncle Hal and Aunt Daisy were tall and dignified and looked alike. A great raconteur, Uncle Hal would tell us numerous stories about his racy ancestors who fought duels for the sake of love, and his experiences in the Boer War and at the Front in the First World War. He was not bitter or disillusioned, but spoke with respect of the wonderful men in his regiment, describing their lives together and inevitably introducing lighter anecdotes. We would sit for hours at his feet in front of the log fire, persuading him to continue. One favourite story told how, as Colonel of his regiment, he had to allocate camels for his men when crossing the desert. Each officer was allowed a strict quota in weight. Uncle Hal used most of his quota on an umbrella and a kitchen chair, dispensing with 'unnecessary clobber', and was surprised to find his batman looking embarrassed as he carefully balanced the chair on top of a hump. It turned out that the NCO's, proud strong men from the mines and mills of Lancashire, had been laughing at their eccentric Colonel. He called the troops together and explained: 'The kitchen chair is essential equipment. I can sit on it when I am tired, stand on it to address you all, and sleep under it to obtain shade.'

Uncle Hal loved playing patience, and an hour before lunch Jane and I would slip into his study (we were not allowed to disturb him before this) and would be initiated into the intricacies of a new game or challenged on an old one. In the afternoons we went for walks, usually in the grounds, or sometimes by the river. Uncle Hal had an uncanny knack of walking with Nature. He knew where to find the hares' burrows and the badgers' setts. He recognised each squirrel, and could tell us how old it was and how large a family it had raised. When he walked through the woods he became lost in his dreams. The birds were never afraid of him. He knew each individual nest and could tell how many generations had used the same nesting-place. He explained in detail how each nest was built, camouflaged and cleaned. Midwife to the birds, he encouraged them to rear their broods in peace. When we walked by the river, he took bearings on each new nest he found and wrote them down in his notebook. He taught us to respect the curlews and moorhens and the wildlife of the water. He knew every pool and bend of the river, the places where fish spawned, and where they could be coaxed to take a line. To him, Nature was constantly alive and exciting.

The grounds of the Hall were beautifully kept. There were no weeds in the gravel paths and herbaceous borders, the lawns were groomed lovingly, the tennis court was smooth. Interlocking greenhouses led to the tropical plant house where orchids, nectarines, figs, palms and grapes grew in a galaxy of colour and foliage. But Jane could only look in from the outside, for this magical environment brought on her asthma. I roamed there alone, breathing in the hot sweet scents of wonder and tasting the fruits of heaven.

On one occasion at Melling, when I was about ten years old, there was a gathering of Boy Scouts and Girl Guides. It was a great event with a band playing, refreshment tents set up in the grounds, and a small platform erected for the presentation of prizes. The pollen count must have been high on that bright summer morning, for Jane was wheezing badly and so was Uncle Hal. After breakfasting alone I was asked to visit him. I found him in bed, propped up with numerous pillows.

'My wife has been called away – I would like you to give the welcoming address. I fear I shan't be able to manage it, I can hardly breathe.'

'No – it's imp-p-possible,' I said weakly. 'I c-c-couldn't do it.' I felt that I would be incapable of controlling my nervous stutter which had developed over the years.

Uncle Hal watched me. I knew he was sympathetic to my distress. He beckoned me to go closer to him, and I sat on the side of his bed. He held my hand and said with difficulty:

'Daphne, you are the only fit person who can represent the family. We invited these people to use our grounds for their celebration. A host must welcome his guests. Remember, it isn't you who matters. Our guests may be nervous or apprehensive, it is up to you to make them relax so that they will enjoy the day. You must give them the freedom of the grounds.' He smiled and looked at the clock by his bed. 'I'm due to speak in ten minutes' time, you have only a moment to comb your hair. Don't forget,' he added, as I slipped off the bed, 'throughout your life, when you meet people for the first time, you must make them relax, then they will be happy. If you are nervous or tense or sullen, your guests will be embarrassed.'

I lost my fear. I made my way to the platform, where the microphone had to be lowered considerably, and I bade them all welcome. It was a most valuable lesson for a ten-year-old.

Melling Hall with all its grandeur – butler, chauffeur, gardeners, domestic staff – was far from typical of the houses in which I stayed during school holidays. They varied considerably, from the very wealthy to the poor, and – more important to me – from the welcoming to the cold. I tried not to outstay my welcome. A two-week visit was enough of an intrusion – for always, even at Melling, I felt myself to be an intruder.

I used to dread my first visit to a new family, but at least I knew that if I did not like the people, or they did not like me, there would be no need for a second encounter. I sympathised with friends who knew no other households apart from their own unhappy or tense families.

There was a place in Glasgow which I visited once with an

unhappy only child. Joy had warned me that her parents were difficult. The house was double-fronted with two main entrance doors, one on either side. When we arrived she said with confidence, 'We can go through Mother's door as Daddy will be working.' Mother and father were staunch Presbyterians who never communicated with each other, but for the sake of their one child remained together to 'give her a home'. They ate in a room that divided the house, each sitting in their own territory, with Joy and myself facing one another on the halfway mark. Joy's bedroom was in the attic – 'It was the only place my parents could agree to,' she said, 'for the room runs over both parts of the house.' Joy spent most of her time alone under the eaves, reading women's magazines. She and her mother found solace in the romantic love stories. When we settled into our beds, Joy's mother and father came up separately, at allotted times, to wish us good night. The only time they were seen as a family was on their Sunday visit to the Kirk – a solemn occasion when Joy walked and sat between her silent parents. There was no rapport. At an early age Joy had become a recluse. She begged me to return for a second visit but selfishly I declined.

Several of the houses I visited were run by young war widows whose married life had been cut short. There was a farm, north of Inverness, to which I went one summer to stay with a friend named Patsy. The house was large and rambling and its lands stretched for miles. Patsy's widowed mother was young, pretty, and greatly respected by her employees. The Scottish sense of loyalty made them serve her with enthusiasm and give of their best. For generations the land had been in the hands of Patsy's family, and the farm workers were not going to desert the good name.

It was here that I learned to ride. I had already been through a course of lessons, but jogging on a wearied mount for an hour once a week could not be compared with riding the free, strong horses at the farm. Patsy had two sisters, and the four of us used to go off for a day's ride. The horses were brought to the front door in the morning, ready saddled, and off we went through woods and forests, over hills and down valleys, wading through rivers and, just occasionally, crossing a road. I was in my seventh heaven. I used to beg for visits to a favourite place, a waterfall deep in the country and difficult to find. Once there we would eat our lunch – home-made sausage rolls still warm from the oven, slices of beef with mustard, whatever Cook had bundled into our hands – and then sink into the damp moss and heather and lie on our backs, staring up at the high trees, and watching the sun catch the water as it sped over the black and grey rocks. We did not talk: the thunderous noise made it difficult to hear, and there was no need of speech.

In the early evening we rode back, exhausted but exhilarated, to watch the shepherds rounding up their flocks and the herdsmen bringing in the cows for milking. We would tumble into the bath, dress again for dinner, and then collapse into bed. Next morning, breakfast in the old farmhouse kitchen: Cook had porridge ready for us – not made with modern, quick-cooking porridge oats but with good, hearty, tasty Scottish grain, which had simmered in the Aga all night long. A large, old-fashioned, yellow mixing-bowl, filled to the brim with thick cream, was set on the breakfast table. We helped ourselves with a heavy silver soup ladle. Instead of syrup or brown sugar, we preferred the bitter-sweet taste of sea salt. Everything was home-made: the bread and baffins which were toasted on top of the cooker, the fresh butter, the jam (raspberry or strawberry), and the thick marmalade with chunks of peel in a runny sharp-tasting liquid. Then we would set out again on a new expedition.

It was in Inverness that I had my first, and only, introduction to blood sports when I joined a local stalk one day. I was at the kill of a magnificent proud stag and to my horror was blooded to commemorate the event. That night I spent hours in the toilet, vomiting, unable to sleep. I could not conceive how so many intelligent and wealthy people could find pleasure in such brutality.

Another friend whose family accepted me was Susan. Her parents had spent the war years in Japanese prison camps and had been involved in building the notorious Siam Railway. They were true blue Scots living in a compact house on the east coast, near Carnoustie. The sitting-room had been turned into a library, with brown leather furniture and anglepoise lamps on reading-tables adding a scholastic atmosphere. 'No talking' was the rule at certain times of the day.

Academic achievement and sporting prowess were the family's mission in life. Susan had three brothers, all athletic. The day began early, sometimes at six o'clock, with a round of golf followed by a quick dip in an ice-cold sea. We ate our breakfast listening to the sports news and whenever possible tuned in to follow the fortunes of the English touring cricket team. Cricket and tennis filled the summer. In winter we drove miles to rugger matches, clutching hot potatoes in our pockets for warmth. By the evening we were physically exhausted, but it was not time for bed. We were taken out, often as far as Aberdeen or Perth, to a concert or an operatic work – but never a ballet for that was considered too effeminate. The family taught me to appreciate art and music. On Sundays we went to the city kirks and listened attentively to a sermon of thirty minutes or more. If a preacher excelled himself, we would return to hear him preach in the afternoon as well. We learned to listen, as each of us had to express an opinion, which was in turn questioned and criticised.

In contrast I used to stay with Mary, a lonely child from a titled family. Her young and lovely mother had experienced a few blissfully happy years of marriage. Then came the war: her husband was reported 'Missing, presumed killed', and she suffered a deep depression from which she never fully recovered. She took no interest in the running of the vast estate her daughter would one day inherit. When the cattle won prizes at Highland shows, she felt no pleasure. When the peacocks displayed their exotic beauty, she did not notice. The estate was the largest and most luxurious I have known, but it meant nothing to her. She was immersed in death.

The house should have rung with laughter and happiness: instead the reception rooms had the shutters closed in the early evenings, the furniture was covered in white sheeting, and large laundry-type bags hung high to enclose the chandeliers. A small study was used as a sitting-room and an upright piano stood in one corner. There was a music room with two Bechstein grands and cupboards full of instruments, but they remained silent. Each morning the maids would feather-dust round the desolate unused rooms, which were filled with cabinets of china while the walls were hung with large family portraits. They opened the windows to allow the fresh air a chance to enter, then quickly closed them again after shaking the curtains. There must have been twenty or more bedrooms, but only two had lights on at night, and fires in the grates lit for comfort. I slept with Mary. The servants were in another wing which I never entered. They wandered about in a ghostly fashion – afraid of being seen. Our meals were served from vast silver dishes by a silent butler, but I cannot remember his serving anything to drink but water. It was a house of silence.

We were allowed to turn over the pages of the large family stamp collection, but forbidden to touch an individual stamp. The dressmaker came once a week for fittings, but the clothes were dark and plain. I do not recall any visitors during the weeks I spent there. I longed to go outside and roam round the farm and gather the eggs in the hay loft and smell the sweetness of the cows being milked, but it was frowned upon, and instead I would disappear and wander round the various closed rooms, looking at newspapers draped on long wooden poles in the smoking-room. The weapons of bygone days stood in a large high-ceilinged hall, guarded by invisible soldiers in the suits of armour. At the end of a long corridor I found a room containing old carriages – landaus, pony traps, victorias, gigs, bassinets – and wooden sleighs. Nearby was a chapel with polished pews, marble coffins and effigies.

My friend had not dared to enter the rooms on her own – I was the first to introduce her to such treasure. She could not remember her father, but from his portraits I could see that there was an uncanny resemblance. Her mother felt that Mary should go to boarding-school for companionship. She was devoted to her daughter in her strange frosty way, perhaps she was frightened of looking at her and finding her husband there. I once went into her bedroom – she slept in a large four-poster bed, and on every high mahogany tallboy there were photographs of her beloved. A shrine facing the window contained a silver tray which held his engraved silver hairbrushes, snuffbox, pipe, silver-handled riding-whip, and other personal possessions. A small red candle-type Eucharist light was kept constantly lit underneath his large portrait.

'Come home with me if you have nowhere to go at Christmas,' said a senior girl whom I hardly knew and certainly rarely had the courage to speak to. She found me one evening in a stone corridor at my school. It was near the end of term, and there had been no invitation for Christmas. My Head Mistress had called me into her study and told me she would arrange for me to go to a holiday home for the first two weeks. Karin was waiting outside, as she had the following appointment, and must have overheard her. 'Mother would love to have you,' she said, and to amplify her statement added, 'she was a missionary doctor in India, so you will have something in common.'

40

We went on the overnight train to London, then changed for Hertfordshire. Dr Mac was one of those old-fashioned, organised yet chaotic, general practitioners, who would do anything for her ill patients, and was sorely tried by others who had little wrong with them but demanded constant attention. Her rambling Victorian house included her surgery, waiting-room and dispensary; next door she had her own maternity home. She worked single-handed and rarely had a full night's sleep as her practice had a radius of twenty miles. Her one luxury was her daily bath, and later she had a telephone installed in the bathroom so that she could relax with a clear conscience.

She was always quick-witted in an emergency. One night when she was speeding across a lonely part of the Fens to visit a dying woman, she saw a car drawn across the road. As she stopped, two masked men approached her. She called out, 'For God's sake move on, the police are after me.' She returned home laughing. 'I've never seen anyone move so fast.'

Two maids helped her run the household and answer the telephones. They were part of the family and utterly devoted to her. She was so involved with her work that for days on end they hardly saw her, leaving her meals to keep warm in a low oven. She ate at any time of the day or night, and I remember finding her eating her lunch at three o'clock in the morning.

On one occasion one of the maids left a note for her saying 'Please tell me when your guest is leaving – for the last four days I have been changing the sheets and towels.' What guest? Dr Mac did not know. She asked the police to keep a watch on the house. 'We have been searching for an escaped prisoner,' they told her. 'We believe he is conducting a series of burglaries in Royston.' It was he who had been the unknown guest. Although Dr Mac had some rare antique silver in her house, none had been stolen. After his re-arrest she visited the prisoner each week until his eventual release.

Another time there was a serious accident outside her front gates. Dr Mac ran out in her dressing-gown and found a young driver pinned under a large American car which had overturned. With enormous effort she managed to lift the chassis sufficiently to release the wounded man. After 'phoning for the ambulance and giving first aid, she accompanied the patient to hospital. Returning home in the early hours of the morning, she found that the crashed car had not yet been removed. Again she tried to lift it –

this time it was impossible. She persuaded us all to go outside and try, but it was far too heavy for us. She had been given unlimited strength at a time of dire emergency.

On Christmas Eve the house was filled with guests. She saw to her last patient at the evening surgery and made sure that her young mothers were settled next door before she came to lead us in the songs and games. We walked with stomachs full and spirits high to Midnight Mass. On Christmas Day she took home-made gifts – food, honey, lavender bags – to the old, the ill or the lonely. There was no humbug about her – she was compassionate and down to earth. It was she who taught me to care for others, and to try to understand the hidden suffering which may lead to difficult behaviour. I envied her children. I wrote to her recently telling her how grateful I had been. 'It never occurred to me that I was giving you anything in those Christmases,' she answered. 'Rather, I was receiving the pleasure of having you. You were an addition to the jollity of the family. I counted you as being one of us.' To her, and to all the people who welcomed me as a stranger, I am eternally grateful.

Whenever I went to visit a new household, three fears worried me. First, did I do my own washing, and if so what soap did I use, and where did I hang the clothes to dry? Secondly, did I make my own bed? If so, did the eiderdown go under the counterpane or on top? Were the blankets folded at the bottom or tucked in? Thirdly, how did I eat my salad? As the guest, I was served first. Did I place the salad on the side-plate, or in the small container (which could also be the finger-bowl), or on the meat plate? I laugh now, remembering those anxieties, but they were very important to me at the time.

I was often pitied – but there was nothing to pity. I was fortunate in having a choice of homes to visit. If there was to be a holiday treat, it was usually kept until I arrived. People were often kind, and for most of the time I was happy. If I did not fit in, I need never return; I was a free agent – yet there were occasions when I longed to belong to someone. I was always part of a family, but never a full member.

My greatest problem was travelling from one place to the next. The opening journey of each holiday was arranged by the school, which bought me a ticket to my first destination, along with those

42

for the other girls who were returning home. I was also given £5 at the start of each holiday. But this money had to cover my expenses throughout the period and pay for my clothes as well. I became a past master at free travel. I would wait for a large family, or better still a group of school children, and I would attach myself to their party. When the ticket collector appeared, I would presume – rightly – that he would not bother to count heads. If I had failed to find a suitable group, I waited until the last moment and then slipped in to the toilet leaving the door slightly ajar, for I knew that if the 'engaged' sign was showing, the ticket collector would knock and wait for an answer. I was never caught.

Clothing, too, was always a difficulty, both schoolwear and mufti. Parents were kind and would offer me second-hand under-wear and casual clothes. I was sometimes allowed to 'pay' for these necessities with clothing coupons or sweet coupons, which were more valuable than money at a time of rationing. I once tried to pay for my railway ticket with a choice of coupons, but the kindly booking-clerk just smiled and said he was unable to bend the rules. I gratefully accepted clothes, but I was too embarrassed to ask my friends to pay for my travel. They were already looking after me free of charge, and besides, if I had asked them for money for my journey, I might not have been given another invitation.

Although I did not know it at the time, my dead father had left a substantial estate. It was governed by Scottish law, and this allowed my mother to claim half (although by the time of his death, he had taken out divorce proceedings). The other half would have provided amply for my expenses. The executors sent the income regularly to Uncle Bob, my official guardian, but he diverted it to his own use. When I reached the age of twenty-one, there was very little of it left.

Uncle Hal – from Melling Hall – thought my financial situation was so unfair that as my twenty-first birthday present he paid for a legal enquiry. The local solicitor advised that nothing could be done.

4

When the East beckons
Follow,
And allow the soul
To unravel.

Coming Out

I met my mother once for a very brief period during my school-days. Sent by car to meet her at the village station, I clutched an old photograph. Yes, I did recognise her from the image of the woman held tightly in my hand, but she walked by me, followed by numerous porters carrying the luggage. Mother had failed to recognise daughter. I was too shy to approach her, but she spoke to me. 'Whose car is that?' she asked; and when I said for whom it had been sent, using her new married name, she exclaimed, 'Good, that's for me' – and mother, stepfather and half-brother stepped into the chauffeur-driven car that had brought me to the station. I was left to walk back to my guardians' where I was finally introduced to the three of them.

When my mother first brought me to England to stay with Uncle Bob and Aunt Maud, I remember taking letters from Ceylon up to her almost daily, and all from the same person. After a few weeks a telegram arrived. The maid was engaged to the postman and I think she must have known the contents, for she asked me to wake my mother, and said that she would bring the breakfast immediately. I thought that the telegram must have brought good news, for my mother's face shone as she said, 'Now all my problems have been solved,' and she quickly left the room to tell the glad tidings to U.B. and A.M.

It was my great-aunt Carrie who retrieved me from the bedroom where I was standing alone. 'Come with me,' she said gently, 'come to my room.' She told me the contents of the telegram: 'Your father is dead,' she said quietly, 'it was very sudden.' She took me into her bed and held me close to her. She knew that

44

she was too old to give me confidence in a future with her, instead she rocked me lovingly in her arms, and her salt tears fell on my face as she whispered over and over again, 'You poor child, may God help you.' The same day my mother made plans to return to Colombo and to the man she eventually married. I was really alone now.

I wrote to her on occasions to tell her what I was doing and where I was going in the holidays. Uncle Hal and Aunt Daisy from Melling Hall wrote several letters to her but had no reply. They thought it strange that a mother failed to take any interest in her daughter's upbringing. One of the Darlington daughters, who was in the Far East, visited my mother, who was then living in Malaya, but she met with a cold reception and was quickly shown to the front door.

'She is not like a mother,' I heard Uncle Hal say, and I have certainly never addressed her by this intimate term, instead I refer to her by her first name.

Even now I know little about her for she did not communicate with her next-of-kin. I was not aware of their existence until I was in my early twenties, when I tried to delve into her history. The result was disillusionment. In recent years I have met her mother, sister, aunt and cousin, who have told me many stories, but they are all hearsay, and I lodge them in the darkest corner of my memory.

After leaving school I had planned to read Medicine, a desire which I longed to achieve. The future seemed bright. I had been independent for years, and there was no reason I could visualise that could interfere with the long years of study. My future career was suddenly shattered by the announcement that I was to go to Singapore to get to know my mother and, more important, so that she could find a husband for me. My plans were dismissed, and I was informed that there was no money available for my dilettantism. Girls were a hindrance but, if respectable, they could be used to advantage socially. It was a waste of time and energy to pore over 'books and bodies', when wine, men and song could be had freely – this was my mother's philosophy.

So I arrived in Singapore, joining my mother and stepfather, and found myself in the gay social life, where one danced the tropical nights away at the Tanglin Club, or swam under the stars in the swimming-pool while the waiters brought dishes of delicious shellfish and jugs of fresh passionfruit juice. I was an addict of both.

It is difficult for people who have lived all their lives in England to understand the importance of 'the Club' to British colonials overseas. It was the centre of all communal and social life. The facilities varied on different stations, but there was always the chance to play one or more sports in the daytime, and to have lunch (usually curry in the Far East); and in the evenings the Club really blossomed, with dinner parties and dances most nights, and people dropping in after dining with friends in their homes. Everything was paid for by signing 'chits', and it was all too easy for newcomers to run up enormous bills without realising it. Nevertheless, to survive in an overseas station, you had to belong to the Club. At some places – and Singapore was one of these – there were several clubs arranged in a strict hierarchy. Membership was not automatic, and it was possible for an applicant to be 'black-balled'. The Tanglin was the summit of every socialite's ambition.

Within days of my arrival I met an unpretentious, handsome young man called Tony, with a beautiful voice and a gift for drawing. He was also an excellent athlete. It was an innocent affair. We were simply happy in each other's company. We used to dance for hours in the tropical night, or drive somewhere quiet to swim. He was everything I longed for. We thought alike – ours was a pure relationship never reaching the perfection of full sexual love, which I now know exists. I was still afraid of sex and he did not force me. As I write this, I try to recall his faults, but I can think of none. He fostered the confidence which I needed; my stutter disappeared at last, returning only when I used the telephone. I did not speak to him about my past, or the relationship which I had with my mother. We had built a peaceful world between us, and I was more than content to exist in it.

Then one day I was summoned by my mother. She was excited. I had accompanied her to an official lunch at Government House, and surprisingly found myself placed next to the Governor. He had been asked to find a suitable young lady to partner a celebrity's son expected on a visit. The day after the luncheon, my mother told me that I was to be given this task. I was not impressed – I had no desire to be away from Tony.

The following day the young man arrived. I had to be his partner at the Tanglin Club. When we met, he had already been at the bottle. Before long, fortified by several stingahs, he insisted on playing the drums in the orchestra. He was hopelessly drunk and it was an outrageous exhibition, tolerated by the Club members only because of his name. I could not sympathise with his humiliation and took him outside where he was promptly sick by the swimming-pool.

For the next few days he was my escort – or to be more accurate, I was his. When he was sober, we escaped the public eye to find a more relaxed atmosphere in Johore Bahru, and I listened to his problems. The only child of a famous man, misunderstood and unhappy, he had built up a jealous hatred of his father and a love for his dead mother which drove him to console himself with drink. Abstemious myself, I found this difficult to accept. I coped with his sickness and begged him to stay sober. In the end, I was happy to be released from the duties of partnering him. I did not see him again.

I do not know whether Tony was angry – he was certainly 'cooler' towards me. It had not dawned on me that he might be upset by my association with another man. Immature as I was, I expected him to be sympathetic. My mother, however, was undoubtedly angry – I had allowed a 'good match' to slip out of my hands. 'A good match?' I queried incredulously: to spend the rest of my life trying to keep someone sober was not my idea of married bliss.

My next major involvement was rather different. I came into the sitting-room one day and found a visitor, a tall, thin, dark-haired man who stood up as I entered, and walked towards me to shake hands. Ralph was an anglophile Frenchman who had worked with SOE in Occupied Europe and was suffering from the consequences. His wealthy father had decided to send him, with a car and chauffeur, on a world-wide tour. For the next two weeks he never left me. He told me that he had had a nervous illness, but that he felt he was improving. He would not sit with his back to the door, and he turned quickly at any unexpected sound, no matter how slight. He was extremely kind, generous, and with impeccable manners. On my birthday he took me to a film première – a light-hearted, happy film starring Danny Kaye. On the way home in his Austin Princess, he closed the glass partition that separated us from the chauffeur.

'I have spoken to your mother,' he told me, 'she has given me permission to ask for your hand in marriage. If you say yes, it will give me great happiness and we will marry immediately – in France, or England, or my father will come to Singapore.'

It was the first time he had held my hand. I said that I was too young, that I did not want to marry yet.

'Please,' he said, 'we will leave it for another two weeks. I will not press you, but I will come every day to see if you will change your mind.'

The following day I went to the Races. Ralph was there. He told my mother what had happened. My mother was furious – I had let slip another good match. She could not contain her anger and struck me across the face, cutting my cheek from my eye to my chin with her large cat's-eye ring When we returned to the house, I was locked in my room, and told that unless I would agree to the marriage, I would remain there; and there I stayed.

Each day at siesta time, 'Cookie' Amah climbed the fire escape to bring me food. 'Cookie' Amah was Chinese, and very beautiful. She and her devoted family were living in Singapore when the Japanese invaded. An officer had the family shot one by one. When it came to Amah's turn to stand in front of the firing squad with her back to a tree, the officer raised his hand and indicated that he would keep her for himself. She had to watch the remaining members of her family die. On her free day each week, Amah and I used to go to this tree and lay sweet perfumed flowers at its roots. Her sadness enhanced her beauty. When male visitors came to the house, she would disappear, for the more vulgar types would imagine that she was easy prey for the cost of a few dollars. I loved her dearly and found comfort with her. She was my link with Ralph. My answer was still 'no', and Ralph left the country.

My love for Tony was as strong as ever, but he had not seen me for some weeks, and I believe now that he had lost his trust in me – certainly at the time I was devastated. My first love has never fully died.

From Singapore my stepfather was transferred to Bangkok in Thailand. I had expected – and hoped – that I would be sent home to England, as 'family' life had been an utter failure. My mother disliked me to such an extent that she would never speak to me directly in normal conversation. My stepfather had to convey the messages. 'Tell Daphne that we shall be going out tonight,' she would say in front of me, and this had to be repeated. I would never respond by being rude or losing my temper, which must have been infuriating. I was a failure in my mother's eyes. I did not live up to her expectations. She had to use threats before I would put on any make-up and, though I wore a little lipstick and powder, I refused to try anything else. I did not want to be married – I felt that I was far too young, and that marriage would mean losing my freedom and independence; but I needed companionship, and this I had. When I look back, I realise that my contemporaries and I shared an innocent time. There were no crude or vulgar jokes. Though we were attracted by the opposite sex, we were not obsessed by sexual activities. Life could be fun and interesting.

Thailand was a beautiful country with its waterways – klongs and floating markets – many of which have now disappeared for ever as they have been turned into highways. Unlike India and Malaya, this was a foreign land to us, and we were guests there, not dictators. The Thais were polite and beautiful. They were justly proud of their culture and crafts – but there was jealousy and cruelty among those in power. Assassination was a constant danger and a common occurrence in high governmental circles.

My private life became increasingly difficult. I relied on two friendly families who would give me a room when I was in need. They were discreet and did not pry into my problems.

I did have one 'escape' from Bangkok society which stands out in my memory. Young, green, hungry for knowledge, I asked the driver to take me up-country to stay with his family – no doubt an unusual request. I wanted to experience a different way of life, to understand something of what made other people 'tick'. The journey lasted about twenty hours. On our way we stopped at a large convent of enclosed nuns, mainly Europeans, who were responsible for about two hundred blind people – some of them children. The young driver opened up the boot of the car, and to my surprise produced the most gaily-coloured cakes iced in vivid greens, oranges and purples. These must have been collected as gifts in celebration of a recent festival. The nuns knew this, and were delighted. Different religions respected one another. I was shown round the primitive buildings, taken to their chapel which was simple and beautiful, given a meal, and blessed by an elderly French priest, before we set off on the journey again.

Late that night, we arrived at a wide meandering river, and drove along the bank for some time. It was the most extraordinary journey, along rough paths with deep pot-holes, and I was afraid that the large American car in which we were driving would break

49

in two – but the driver insisted that all was well, and all would be well; and so it was. We caught sight of a mass of teak logs floating down-river. They were lashed together and had small shelters for protection against the sun or monsoon. This was the family's temporary 'home'. The driver hailed the people who were sitting comfortably on the logs, and they drew to the side of the river. There was a welcome as I was led aboard. The driver waved goodbye.

I expected to settle down with the women for the night, but first they led me across the logs to the men's section. Later on during the journey I found that the routine was the same every evening. The women would cook a meal in their own section and carry it across the logs to join the menfolk; they would eat together, and then the men would take out their long opium pipes. The women sat beside them and filled their pipes with the drug (I do not recollect seeing any of the women smoke). It never occurred to me to try my hand at smoking opium, but with the other women I sat and filled the pipes. The atmosphere was calm and relaxed. It was over thirty years ago, and memory may fail me, but I recall nothing but tranquil happiness, all through that journey. The ten days or so that it took us to float down-river to the estuary were one of those rare times that I felt one with Nature – the peace and beauty of the jungle environment overwhelmed me.

Eventually my stepfather's tour of duty in Thailand came to an end, and we returned to England on furlough. My mother did not speak a word to me for the whole journey until we arrived at the Cumberland Hotel in London. There she turned to me and said, 'We are staying here for a few days – goodbye.' I telephoned the Darlingtons from a call-box, and they immediately welcomed me to their home. I became so much a part of their family that Aunt Daisy presented me at Court with Jane.

Marriage

I soon readjusted to living in England and, after a happy time with the Darlingtons, I began to think of my future. Dr Mac's daughter Karin, my old friend from school, had been studying Science for two years (we had not been taught Science subjects at school) and hoped to take her 'A' levels and then go to Edinburgh to read Medicine. Dr Mac had offered to look after me if I wished to follow suit – but the East had intervened, and I was two years behind.

I went to stay with a girl whose father was a dentist in Bedford. She suggested that I might talk to her father. He tried to persuade me to read Dentistry. However, one weekend I met one of his patients – Mrs Hitchcock, the widow of the late rector of St Botolph's, Cambridge. She was told of my plight and immediately offered accommodation at the rectory. She had had a gingivectomy and some extractions and was too ill to drive. I had never driven a car before, yet I found myself behind the wheel of her erratic old Austin, while she gave me my first driving-instructions with her mouth full of blood-stained cotton wool. So began yet another strange period in my life.

St Botolph's Rectory had numerous rooms – all of them rented by undergraduates. Mrs Hitchcock lived in a small wooden shed in the garden. She took me up to a bedroom facing the drive.

'Here you are, you can have this room – I hope you will be comfortable.'

She was a sweet lady with fluttering eyelids. The next morning she came in with a breakfast tray.

'I am spoiling you today – you look tired out. Did you sleep well?' she added.

'Yes, I slept beautifully.'

'Oh, good. The last person to sleep in your bed committed suicide last week; he cut his throat, it made a dreadful mess, but I bought a new mattress, though the stain is still on the divan underneath.' And so it was.

I had been despondent and a little frightened when I set out for Cambridge, but now I felt happier. I was accepted by the local Technical College to study Science 'A' levels, which they hoped I would be able to complete in one year. To pay for my living expenses I served early-morning breakfasts at The Whim restaurant and in the evening I helped with dinners at the University Arms Hotel. It meant two free meals a day, so there was no need to spend money on food. My doctor, Edward Bevan, arranged an interview for me with the local educational authority, and I was astounded to be given a grant. I spent part of the interview promising to give back any money which might be made available to me. The members of the committee must have thought I was unusual. However, I am still surprised that no government in Britain has asked students to reimburse their university grants. They would surely appreciate their studentship more, working with extra enthusiasm and taking a pride in their achievements. Several European countries, and Japan, have sensibly arranged a long-term repayment system, once a graduate is established in a job and earning a salary.

Socially, I was spoilt at Cambridge. Mrs Hitchcock surrounded me with kindness. My spell in the Far East had accustomed me to the gaieties of youth and I was used to living in a male-dominated society. I was happy to be amongst so many contemporaries who were not straight from school, as National Service was still compulsory. The majority had tasted the fruits of freedom, and some of them had known fear.

In May Week, 1954, I accepted invitations for all three nights of May Balls. The setting was the most perfect in the world, the breath-taking beauty of the colleges surrounded by the natural majesty of the trees and gardens. In the early morning we would punt on the tranquil River Cam, passing under the weeping willows on the Backs, and make towards Grantchester Meadows to eat breakfast in the dew of the orchards.

My medical ambitions did not get very far. I was due to take my 'A' levels in the summer of 1955, and hoped to start reading Medicine in the following October, but I met John.

Before going up to Cambridge, John had spent two years in the Army doing his National Service. He was fortunate enough to spend a large part of the time in a German hotel, as being a good games player he was selected to swim for his regiment. He trained in the hotel's Olympic-sized swimming-pool and participated in Finnish-style baths, being 'flayed' and then plunging into ice-cold water. After three years at Cambridge, taking his degree in History, he was undecided about his career, so read for a Diploma in Education.

He spent a term at Fettes School in Edinburgh, and during that time I had constant telephone calls saying that schoolmastering was definitely not for him. The Head Master at Fettes was known to invite the younger masters to lunch on Sunday and afterwards, if the weather was fine, he might mount his horse and expect the masters to follow him on foot. John was unused to this sort of exercise and the hearty exuberance of such a bucolic crowd of boys was too much to cope with. At the end of this period, he was still unsure of his future.

From Fettes he returned to Cambridge for his last term, and went for an interview thinking he might join M.I.5. He would have been a hopeless agent as he is incapable of keeping a child's birthday present a secret.

The Cambridge Appointments Board sent him numerous other suggestions for a future career. He applied for one, a Head of History post at a school in the south of England, and to our amazement he was offered the position before he left the interview. The following day he wrote declining it, on the basis that the school must be in a run-down state if a new graduate was to be appointed as Head of Department.

Either out of frustration, or by mistake, the Appointments Board sent details of a post at Harrow School. 'Required – a Mathematics Master to teach in Junior forms – an interest in Games an advantage.' John applied for fun; he had 'O'-level Maths to his credit. He was offered an interview to which he completely forgot to go. Dr James, the Head Master, wrote offering him a second interview the following week, and mentioned

53

casually that there had been so many applicants that he would have to make a decision immediately.

The Head Master and two senior mathematicians, John Morgan and Kenneth Snell, interviewed John one afternoon. He was immediately appointed to the staff, with a promise that he would be transferred to the History Department when a vacancy arose.

John had asked me to marry him before – in a vague sort of way – and to his letter accepting the Harrow appointment he added a postscript announcing our engagement, but continuing: 'We do not intend to get married for some time yet.' When I mentioned my medical ambitions, John's reply was: 'We will have six children first while we are young, and when the sixth goes to school, then you can start on your university career.' I took him at his word.

Meantime there was the problem of Maths. We made our way to Dillon's Bookshop and bought an excellent revision book which had been produced by the War Office for the Forces. Each evening was spent revising for the following day's lessons. By joint effort (for I had a higher Maths qualification than John) we just managed to keep one step ahead of the boys. No one found out how limited John's mathematical ability really was. Recently when we were walking down Oxford Street, an Old Harrovian greeted us and introduced John to his friend as 'the best Maths teacher I ever had'. The best brains do not always make the best masters. This particularly applies in the scientific field. It is often easier to teach a subject which one has just mastered, as the problems solved are fresh in one's mind.

I visited Harrow on several occasions during John's first term, and liked what I saw. The village of Harrow on the Hill consists mostly of school buildings, with a few small shops. It is said that Henry VIII's hunting-lodge once stood on the site of the popular King's Head Hotel which is renowned for its good food and comfort. At the top of The Hill, partially hidden from view by trees, is the great church of St Mary's. Archbishop Lanfranc laid her foundation stone in 1087 and the building was consecrated by his successor, Anselm, in 1094. The saint and martyr Thomas à Becket worshipped in this church – his last visit was in December 1170 before travelling to Canterbury where 'this turbulent priest', as Henry II described him, was murdered on December 29.

At the foot of The Hill, quite separate from the village, is

Harrow town, out of bounds for the boys in our day. Town dwellers refer to the village as 'The Hill'.

The school was virtually an island hanging high over London. It was surrounded by trees and fields, and could boast a lake in the middle of a wooded glen. I remember arriving early one day and deciding to make a tour of my own whilst waiting for John. London was only eleven miles away – so near – yet standing at the top of The Hill, and looking towards the great city, it seemed a world apart. I watched the squirrels preparing for their hibernation, collecting their early nuts of the autumn. There was evidence of moles and badgers, and there were birds of different hues. The cows from the school farm strolled in the lush fields and there were fish to be caught in the lake. Nature was still undisturbed in the countryside. There was a haze over London in the days before the city was made into a smokeless zone, and this cut The Hill still further away from the metropolis.

On the following Saturday I went again to Harrow and stood on the touchline watching a rugger match. John, who had captained the Cambridge LX Club, was standing, whistle in hand, refereeing the First XV. It was a dry autumn day, the trees had started to shed their leaves, and there was the smell of bonfires. The sun glowed through the haze turning the oaks and chestnuts a rich golden-brown. Masters' children laughed as they ran to catch the whirling leaves which danced in the breeze, making their final farewell to life before dying and re-entering the earth.

Harrow took games seriously. House matches were as important as school matches for the boys and their housemasters. I was an old hand at being a rugger spectator and felt quite at home, surrounded by masters and their families, and hundreds of boys eager to cheer. Some of the masters, like John, were in rugger gear; others were in casual clothes – some over-casual, with flat caps and Hawks' ties and, despite the warmth of the afternoon, 'full blue' scarves. The only person who seemed to be on his own was the Head Master, Dr R. L. James, known as 'Jimmy James'. He was dressed in his grey suit, with his trousers tucked into his wellingtons, a hat on his head, and his dog beside him. He was obviously enjoying the match and interested in what the boys were doing, but did not allow himself to show much enthusiasm. His wife, Bobbie, stood talking to some old boys who had escaped from London for the day.

Were all my future Saturdays to be spent watching from the

touchline or the running-track, lounging in a deck chair by the cricket pavilion, sitting on the grass by the swimming-pool – depending on the season? Was I to join the hearty 'hallo there' group of adolescent adults, whose personalities were transformed by the very mention of any sport? I stood glassy-eyed and trembling to think that in twenty years' time, I might be standing on the same spot watching a future generation playing on the same pitch, and holding a fixture list with the names of the same public schools.

My daydream was brought to an abrupt end by a housemaster pushing in front of me to shout:

'Come on House. You're not offside. Take no notice of the ref! He can't see properly. Run boy!'

John blew a long – a very long – blast on the whistle. The game stopped, the boys rested on their haunches or sank to the ground glad of the break. The crowded touchline fell quiet in anticipation. John walked towards us frowning and stopped a few yards in front of the housemaster.

'I am the referee,' he said firmly but calmly. 'Either you keep quiet or I shall order you off the field.'

For a moment, senior housemaster and young beak stood facing one another. Everyone nearby was quite still, stunned by John's defiance of the hierarchy and far too interested in the outcome to move or speak. Far away – it seemed – other House matches continued but the cheers and counter-cheers were faint.

The housemaster said nothing. After a while he turned on his heel and strode away. John walked back to the centre of the field and blew a short blast. The boys rose a little wearily. The game re-started.

'That's Johnnie Rae,' said a lanky boy standing beside me, the collar of his 'bluer' turned up and his shallow straw boater tipped forward over his forehead. 'He's the new Maths beak. Have you heard that he's getting married to a woman from the Far East? He told us she was born in Ceylon.'

'I wonder what shade she will be,' said another boy, stockier than his companion.

The first boy tilted his head back so that he could see the game under the rim of his boater. 'Coffee,' he said authoritatively.

'It's all very well having Eastern princes as Harrovians,' said the second boy, 'but it's pushing it a bit far bringing in a coloured wife.'

56

The first boy was quiet for a while, but then the explanation must have occurred to him. 'He wasn't at Harrow,' he said.

'Who?'

'The new beak.'

The second boy nodded in silence. There was nothing more to be said.

That was my introduction to Harrow.

★ ★ ★

We decided to ask Murray Irvine to officiate at our Cambridge wedding. He was the College chaplain at Sidney Sussex, and one of the few people John respected in the Church. From childhood I had had a premonition that my wedding-day would be on New Year's Eve – and so it was. Saturday, December 31, 1955, was the only day that Murray could manage. He then shocked us by saying that the College Chapel was not licensed for marriages, so we would either have to pay £75 to Lambeth Palace, or have a civil wedding at a register office first. Unable to justify myself paying £75 to satisfy an outdated law, and holding that no sheet of paper could sanctify a religious ceremony, I chose the latter course. I had a 'phone call from John to say that he had been to see the registrar at Harrow, and had arranged for us to go through the civil ceremony on December 17. 'No need to bring any witnesses, the registrar said he could arrange for someone to be present. It only takes twenty minutes, and I have a free period after Break, so I should be able to fit it in. I'll meet you outside the classroom – don't be late.'

December 17 found me in a borrowed tartan skirt, and a long, navy blue, polo-necked sweater of John's. A recent fire had destroyed my wardrobe, and never having been fashion-conscious, I had decided to spend what little money I had on a few necessary articles with which to set up a home. John told me that he would transfer his bank balance from Lloyds to my account at the Midland Bank. My ego was satisfied, but I felt thoroughly deflated on receiving a bank statement with a total in red: '£3 17s. 6d.' – John had in fact transferred his overdraft. I remained calm when I collected my fiancé in his gown and mortar board.

My sweater slipped further down my slim body as I got out of the car, and was nearly the same length as the borrowed tartan skirt.

'Happy wedding-day, darling,' he said, 'you look wonderful. We're due in five minutes – so put your foot down.'

Mid-morning traffic in Harrow is chaotic on Saturdays. While I parked the car, John rushed into the bleak register office to announce our arrival. When I reached the door I found John doing battle with the registrar, who took one look at my outrageous clothing and burst out:

'This isn't a joke. Where are your guests?' he spluttered. 'You haven't brought any witnesses. I won't marry you. And I haven't another free date until the New Year. Go away now, I can't argue further, there are others waiting.'

A shy elderly couple came into the room and sat down.

'Are you getting married today?' I asked.

'No, we have come to put up our banns.'

'Please,' I begged, 'will you witness our marriage?' and they did.

The registrar was furious, the couple were kind though startled. I shook with nerves all through the ceremony and could not remember a word that was said. A pen was thrust into my hands, I signed a paper, and with relief I made for the door.

'Oh no you don't,' said the registrar, 'I'm not having your pictures in the local paper. You use *this* door.' And he ushered us out into the back yard.

★ ★ ★

Our second marriage occurred as planned on New Year's Eve. The sun shone and the day was warm. The winter sales had started, and we spent the morning trying to find John a waistcoat. We called at a shop we had visited some months earlier, the day John first proposed marriage to me. He had insisted then that I accompany him for the last fitting of his rugger blazer – a beautiful maroon garment with a gold lion rampant on the pocket. It was a perfect fit. I exclaimed my approval to the delighted tailor who proceeded to fold the jacket.

'My fiancée will write out the cheque,' said John.

I was so dumbfounded at the word 'fiancée' that I meekly paid the bill. There was no further reference made to this new relationship for some months.

The same tailor sold us the wedding-day waistcoat and, as he wrapped it, asked how we were enjoying married life.

'We have two hours to go until the marriage ceremony,' I laughed, and we walked arm in arm out of the shop.

We had decided to have an early lunch at the Red Lion pub, and on the way passed a hairdressing shop. I saw several of my six bridesmaids sitting under the dryers. I had rarely been to the hairdresser's (even now, in middle age, I use a pair of cutting-out scissors and wash under a shower) and it had never occurred to me that my hair would need any special treatment on my wedding-day. I rushed by the window hoping that I had not been seen, as my bridesmaids would have disapproved of my ultra-casualness.

Murray Irvine had kindly offered me his College rooms in which to change into my white velvet wedding-dress. Miss Perrin, an old and eccentric dressmaker, was already there, sitting at the sewing-machine with pieces of velvet lying all over the floor.

'I have 'flu, Daphne, my temperature's well over a hundred degrees. Hurry and have a fitting.'

It was a quarter to two, and the service was at three o'clock.

Brother Peter Searle, a Franciscan friar from the monastery at Cerne Abbas, and another of the few churchmen whom John respected, was the best man. He was beautifully turned out in a new habit specially made for the occasion, even including a small pocket designed to hold the wedding-ring.

At three o'clock I painfully walked up the aisle, cutting the skin of my ankles on the pins which were holding up the hem of my dress. It was so painful that I had asked the bridesmaids to walk in front of me, so that I should not be seen to be limping. Matters did not improve when I left a shoe behind on a step in the middle of the aisle, and had to retrace my steps, to the surprise of Malcolm Carter, the friend who was giving me away. He thought that I was having second thoughts and making for the door.

After the horror of the register-office ceremony, the beauty of the church service was a marked contrast – made even more so by the love and care with which Murray conducted it. We both knew him well, and he drew our guests together as a family. His sermon was wise and to the point, and although I was calm, I was filled with emotion. The only hiatus came when Brother Peter could not find the new pocket that held the wedding-ring, and virtually disrobed as he searched the various folds of his habit trying to locate it.

The Sidney Sussex chef had organised a superb reception in

College Hall. This was, I think, a gift from the College as the bill, inclusive of wine and champagne, came to £46 for a hundred and thirty people, negligible by any standards. We were very poor – too poor to afford flowers for College Hall as well as the Chapel, so the same lot had to do for both, and while the guests were being photographed, the ushers could be seen frantically rushing the huge vases from Chapel to Hall.

We were the first to leave the reception and, after a quick change, drove out to a little café on the outskirts of Cambridge. We had just ordered crumpets and a pot of coffee in front of the log fire, when the door opened and in walked one of the guests, John's old tutor, still dressed in his tailcoat. We relaxed and laughed.

We planned to return to Cambridge for a honeymoon at the Blue Boar Hotel. We were rather surprised when we walked into the dining-room that evening to find it filled with dozens of wedding-guests who had decided to stay on for the New Year in this beautiful town. It was as much of a surprise to them as it was to us. Glasses were raised, jokes were made, and I decided to eat my first-ever oysters. I cannot find words to describe the feel of them in my mouth, and after forcing down half a dozen, I had to retreat to the toilet to allow them to return.

At lunch next day, a young Harrovian, Hugh Cameron-Rose, recognised us. He decided that we should be his companions during the rest of our stay in Cambridge. There was no escape.

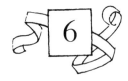

Harrow

There is evidence that a school existed at Harrow in the fifteenth century, and Mary Tudor, Queen from 1553 to 1558, is known to have sent some of her protégés to a school in 'Church House' on The Hill; but the man who is generally credited with the foundation of the modern Harrow School is John Lyon, who in 1571 obtained a charter from Elizabeth I:

'Whereas our beloved subject John Lyon of the parish of Harrow on the Hill in our County of Middlesex, a yeoman inspired by divine grace with the instinct of charity, has resolved to found, create, and for ever to establish anew in the town of Harrow on the Hill in our County of Middlesex a certain Grammar School with one schoolmaster and one usher for the perpetual education, training and instruction of boys and youths of the said parish and generously to endow and maintain two scholars in our University of Oxford; and has determined to repair and mend at his own very great expense certain highways between Edgware and London as well as in other places; and (to undertake) further works of devotion and piety for the very great benefit and encouragement of the scholars applying themselves to learning in the said parish; thereby offering a very good example to all other to imitate the like hereafter; and also for the common profit of all our subjects – '

Lyon was a wealthy landowner, and the school he endowed still owns over 300 acres in Harrow itself, besides Shepherd Market in London's Mayfair.

The school was to provide free education for local scholars and the Governors were to be prominent men of that parish. Lyon ordered that they 'shall not receive any girl into the said school'. Originally Harrow provided education only for day boys; now, however, it is rare for day students to be accepted. The school still does not cater for girls.

From modest beginnings Harrow School has grown to 740 boys, divided among eleven Houses, and taught by over seventy full-time staff. The boarding-houses are separate buildings scattered over The Hill. They have their own individuality and a housemaster is – in the opinion of many – as important to the young boy as a headmaster.

I am reminded of Sir Arnold Lunn's autobiography, *Come What May*. He was at Harrow from 1902 to 1907. The House he went to was called 'The Knoll', and had just been taken over by the Rev. E. C. E. Owen:

'It was the worst House in the school when he took charge, and perhaps the best House when he handed it over many years later to his successor. It had a bad name for bullying, and one of those, now dead, who helped to create a veritable reign of terror among the small fry figured later in a German report compiled by way of retort to the Bryce Report on atrocities. He was accused by the Germans of ill-treating their prisoners.'[4]

When John went to Harrow, in the autumn of 1955, shortly before our marriage, housemasters were appointed by seniority, and could not remain in office for more than fifteen years (often, being older men, they reached their official retiring age before this). During their period in the House, the men were a law unto themselves, and ruled their domains in very different styles. They lived virtually free of charge. Food, gas, electricity, laundry and domestic arrangements would all be covered. Gardeners cared for the magnificent House grounds and kept the tennis courts in top condition. It was natural that many masters (though not all) would wait anxiously to be offered such a position. 'Once appointed,' as the Harrovian novelist H. A. Vachell wrote, 'it is almost as difficult to turn an Eton or Harrow master out of his House as to turn a parson of the Church of England out of his pulpit.'

A new housemaster was named a year or two in advance of his predecessor's retirement. Tension mounted as the time for the announcement grew closer. There was anxiety and rivalry among those who were high on the list, and of course, this affected their families. Each invitation to dine at the Head Master's house was seen as indicating a chance of being chosen, and hours were spent in preparing a meal in return.

Appointments to housemasterships were entirely at the Head Master's discretion. Masters tried to prove themselves by winning prestige and improving their place in the hierarchy. To teach the Sixth was a step up for a junior master; to be Head of a subject, such as French or German, was to achieve a higher grade under the Head of Modern Languages. The same applied in the Science field: the Head of Science was higher up the ladder than the Head of Biology. Besides the Heads of Department – Classical, Art, History, etc. – there was the Head of the Timetable – an important but frustrating position, as this man was responsible for replacing sick masters at a moment's notice. All these positions are vital if the school is going to be well run. There were also prestige jobs on the sports side – to run the cricket, rugger, Harrow football, swimming and athletics. Another important role was being in charge of the Harrow School Boys' Club – the club which they financed and helped to run in the old Paddington slums. It was unusual to be paid extra for a 'prestige' position, even if this should involve many hours of hard work.

The situation would be difficult enough if schoolmasters were perfect human beings – but they are not. Many of the difficulties which arise in the relationships between masters and boys can be better understood if it is accepted that some of the masters in a single-sex boarding school may themselves be very immature, and in fact have been drawn back into the environment of their childhood and adolescence in search of security. This does not mean that they are not good schoolmasters – on the contrary, they may have a deeper understanding than the fully mature and self-assured man. However, there is a dangerous element too, of which the master may not be aware. He may desperately want to impress the boys, to be continually revered, or vie for popularity. The young man fresh from university, the senior members of the common room, including housemasters, and sometimes even the headmaster: all are liable to fall into this trap, though usually oblivious of the role they are playing.

Recently I saw a letter from a schoolmaster to an ex-pupil who had left boarding-school after a few unhappy terms; and the emotions it revealed illustrate this point so vividly that I will quote some sentences from it. The master began by saying that he had been 'greatly saddened' by the boy's departure:

'I used to enjoy so much our chats in the corridor from time to time and I like you, even though I thought your Biology was not far short of downright disgraceful. I presume you have left because your father has realised that this school is a pretty bad school these days. . . . I confess that I am wholly in agreement with him.'

He went on to speak of a previous headmaster under whom 'Biology really thrived'. But then:

'X was given the push and we were landed with that dreadful, slimy drip Y as Head Master who let the school disintegrate academically; and Science, in particular, collapsed. Now we have Z who is letting the school Science sink even further into the abyss. The difference between them is that Y was unlikeable but, in a strange way, slightly lovable, whereas Z is likeable but totally unlovable. And the school continues to slide, with ever increasing acceleration, into the bottomless pit.'

He urged the boy to write, saying that he was most anxious that they should keep in touch 'for many a year to come. I miss your friendly, genial company here so much.' By any standards this was a most strange letter, combining as it does a complete lack of loyalty to the headmaster and an obvious attempt to curry favour with the boy. I asked if there had been any attempt at a homosexual relationship; apparently not, though the letter strongly suggests to me that the inclination was there. The boy feared and disliked the master intensely, and this was a contributing factor in the general unhappiness which had made him want to leave.

The impact of jealous masters trying to gain popularity may have devastating results. Adolescent boys are searching for perfection; they want to model themselves on a character they admire, and where better to find a variety of choice than in the confines of a boarding-school? A young boy may see a jovial master, who is generous with his affection and time, and decide that this is the man he wishes to emulate. But there is the other kind.

I knew a bachelor housemaster at a well-established school who longed for recognition and popularity among the 'right' members of his house. He had been conscripted during the war, and refused to give up his Army rank in peacetime. He was discharged at his 'acting' rank, one rung higher than the substantive rank he had achieved. He needed the psychological security of this rank, and was in fact known by it. He was fond of the bottle, and so were some of the boys whom he wished to influence. They would share an alcoholic evening, ending on occasions by making lurid telephone calls to women, including the headmaster's wife. An exhibitionist and homosexually inclined, he would pick on the more unfortunate boys in his house, who were made to wash his back in the bath. On one occasion he was asked to allow a girl of sixth-form age to spend the night in his spare room. She found her bed filled with inflated balloons, and woke up during the night to find him standing at its foot (he left at once). The boys accepted him, and played up to his whims – they could use him as much as he could use them. His activities were so blatant that he was treated as a joke – but do parents pay for 'joke' housemasters?

Another incident which illustrates the effects of jealousy and popularity-seeking occurred to me at Harrow. John was refereeing the First XV match, and I had parked my car outside our garage. A master who was senior to John, but who was in charge of a more junior game – thus making him feel inferior – decided that the position of my car threatened 'his' turning-circle for his car. He retaliated by smearing my car with cow dung to the accompaniment of sycophantic laughter from some of the boys, most of whom were embarrassed.

Schoolmasters may have favourites amongst their pupils for a variety of reasons. The chosen boys may be good-looking, or academically bright, or have athletic ability. A master may see in a favourite boy reminders of his own youth, and through him retrace his steps to his own school days. There is much make-believe among masters in an all-male boarding-school.

For a man to be confident in his relationships with women, it is necessary for him to be confident in relationships with his fellow men. Some schools will only accept married men for house-master- or headmasterships, and knowing this, masters may well choose marriage partners on Platonic terms. Many remain dedicated bachelors, and like dedicated bachelor priests they devote their lives to their vocation. It is difficult to fault such men in their roles as housemasters or headmasters.

If he becomes over-influenced by the immature type of master, a public-school boy may remain a public-school boy for life, and although he may hold a responsible position in one of the professions, he remains emotionally childish and immature in his personal relationships – so much so that he has few, if any, friends. He is too afraid of giving anyone the power to break down his make-believe barriers.

The young and the old need heroes. Young boys develop their

personalities by observing those around them, and comparing one character with another. Boarding-school education has the advantage of providing a wider range of possible 'models' in day-to-day life. Masters and staff will be seen at work and at leisure, and in their family or bachelor environment, and offer a variety of comparisons, from the academic to the athletic. Boys living at home naturally imitate their fathers; in boarding-school they find that the spectrum is greatly enlarged. They can explore their own hidden potentialities, and may be surprised to find their own characters form and mature into manhood as they consciously – or unconsciously – emulate those whom they respect.

There are many good masters who progress up the ladder to housemaster, or even headmaster. At the same time, there are assistant masters who do not want to take part in the hierarchical system – men who are mature emotionally and in their personal relationships, and who are the backbone of all public schools. It is they who will influence the more stable boy, it is they who stand out among their contemporaries in the common room, free of jealousy or hang-ups. They do exist.

House life at Harrow varied with the housemaster. Nowadays a housemaster has a house tutor to help him, but in the nineteen-fifties, with the exception of such assistance as the house matron might give, he, and he only, stood *in loco parentis* to all boys in his House, both with regard to education and upbringing. The standards of the housemaster were the standards of the House. In choosing an appropriate House for their son, parents relied on the impression they gained from the housemaster. On the whole, the Head Master took care, when appointing a new housemaster, to continue the tradition of that particular House – thus there were Houses which were predominantly 'aristocratic', 'games-y', 'intellectual', or a combination of these.

One characteristic was shared by all Houses: they were extremely sociable. We were often invited to House dinner parties after which the guests – always in full evening dress – were led into the boys' dining-room to sing House songs. Most of these songs were sentimental, and I enjoyed them immensely. At the end of the evening, we usually sang one of my favourites, with a soft nostalgic tune:

Good night! Ten o'clock is nearing –
Lights from Hampstead, many, fewer, more,
Fainter, fuller, vanishing, appearing,
Flash and float a friendly greeting o'er;
    Read them, read them
    Ere the slumber come –
    God will speed them
    Here across the gloom;
All good comes to those who read aright –
See they are twinkling, Good night, Good night.

Good night! What shall follow after?
Wish great play, and vigour ever new.
Wish for race and merriment and laughter –
Hampstead lights must surely wish it too.
    Luck befriend thee
    From the very toss –
    See, they send thee
    Victory across –
Speed the ball, and animate the fight:
So, till the morning, Good night, Good night.

The history of Harrow's songs goes back to the time of the
Reverend H. Montagu Butler, DD, Head Master from 1860 to
1885. The School Song Book is dedicated to this Head Master,
'under whose encouragement SINGING has become part of our
school life'. Montagu Butler was the tenth and youngest child of
George and Sarah Butler, and in becoming Head Master he
followed his father's example for George Butler had been Head
Master from 1805 to 1829. Montagu was himself a student at the
school and to date is the only Old Harrovian to become Head
Master. Perhaps his Alma Mater period was a happy one, for he
was so anxious to follow in his father's footsteps that he produced
thirty-two testimonials to impress the Governing Body prior to
his election. He was well versed in the problems and loneliness of
headmastership. His grandfather, the Rev. Wheedon Butler, was
yet another headmaster; and an uncle, William Oxenham, was an
assistant master at Harrow. Another family connection of great
interest lay in his sister-in-law, Josephine Butler, who devoted a
major part of her life to combating regulated prostitution. She also
fought against the Contagious Diseases Act. A brave woman
indeed.

Amongst Montagu Butler's students were one archbishop

(Lord Davidson), seventeen judges, four viceroys of India, sixty-four generals, the novelist John Galsworthy, and the Prime Minister Stanley Baldwin (described as 'a man who somewhat uniquely played the game of politics as though it were cricket'). 'When the call came to me to form a government,' Baldwin said, 'one of my first thoughts was that it should be a government of which Harrow should not be ashamed. I remembered how in previous governments there had been four or perhaps five Harrovians, and I determined to have six.'

During Montagu Butler's term in office 'House Singing' was introduced, and was to become an important feature of school life, encouraged by Butler himself and by his successor, J. E. C. Welldon, Head Master from 1885 to 1898.

The words of the first songs were written by E. E. Bowen, an assistant master at Harrow from 1859 to 1901. He was renowned as an athlete, and had enormous influence on athleticism at the school. Bowen's desire was to enshrine for ever Harrow's traditions. According to his nephew, twenty-six of Bowen's songs were devoted wholly or largely to games.

In 1888 when F. S. Jackson saved the school at the Eton and Harrow match by taking, in all, eleven wickets, and scoring 80 runs (21 in the first innings, 59 in the second), the Head Master, Welldon, gave Bowen three days' leave to compose a song commemorating the event. The result was 'A Gentleman's a-Bowling':

> *Light Blue are nimbly fielding,*
> *And scarce a hit can pass;*
> *But those the willows wielding*
> *Have played on Harrow grass.*
> *And there's the ball a-rolling,*
> *And all the people see*
> *A gentleman's a-bowling –*
> *And we're a-hitting he!*

Bowen's songs were set to music by the organist John Farmer. The two of them must share the credit for many favourite songs. Others, too, followed, writing songs intended to induce love of games, school and country in their singers. The patriotic feeling instilled in the boys never left them. The camaraderie, the sense of belonging to a team and a House, were extended to embrace the school and, eventually, the country and the empire. This patriotic feeling was nurtured by songs such as Henry Newbolt's 'Play Up and Play the Game'. The singing of 'House Songs' culminated once a year in 'School Songs', held in Speech Room, when a whole philosophy of life was summed up by such songs as '1885', dedicated to E. M. Butler, Captain of the Harrow Football XI, and written by E. M. Howson, a colleague of Edward Bowen:

> They tell us the world is a scrimmage,
> And life is a difficult run,
> Where often a brother shall finish
> A victory we have begun.
> What matter, we learnt it at Harrow,
> And that was the way that we won.

Harrovians were known to get together in deepest Africa or on the Indian tea plantations, sitting on the verandas of their colonial bungalows and, with no doubt a glass of whisky in one hand and a good meal in their stomach, letting their voices rise to tell the world:

> When Raleigh rose to fight the foes,
> We sprang to work and will;
> When glory gave to Drake the wave,
> She gave to us The Hill.
> The ages drift in rolling tide,
> But high shall float the morn
> A-down the stream of England's pride
> When Drake and we were born!
> For we began when he began,
>   Our times are one;
> His glory thus shall circle us
>   Till time be done.

Among Welldon's pupils was Winston Churchill, whose mother corresponded regularly with the Head Master – they were both determined that young Winston should pass his exams and go to Sandhurst. Sadly they were to be disappointed; the young man failed, and had to go on to a crammer after his sojourn at Harrow. It was not through lack of trying. He loved the English language, he wrote eloquent letters and had the gift of wit (when a newly appointed master asked despairingly of his class, 'What am I to do with boys who know nothing?' the young Churchill replied: 'Please, Sir, teach us'): but he was a late developer. Churchill became an ardent supporter of 'School Songs'. He attended throughout the Second World War and in the post-War years (his last appearance at 'Songs' was in 1961, four years before his death), and was seen to be deeply moved, retracing his student days when with five hundred fellow Harrovians he sang with such determination, vowing to his school and country that he would emulate the great deeds of the past:

> Guard, guard it well, where Sidney fell,
> The poet-soldier's grave,
> Thy life shall roll, O royal soul,
> In other hearts as brave.
> While thought to wisdom wins the gay,
> While strength upholds the free,
> Are we the sons of yesterday,
> Or heirs of thine and thee?

For 'School Songs' on December 18, 1940, a master, Edward V. C. Plumptre, wrote an additional verse to 'Stet Fortuna Domus':

> Nor less we praise in darker days
> The leader of our nation,
> And CHURCHILL's name shall win acclaim
> From each new generation.
> While in this fight to guard the Right
> Our country you defend, Sir,
> Here grim and gay we mean to stay,
> And stick it to the end, Sir.

The following year Churchill commented on the first line of this new verse, saying, 'I have obtained the Head Master's permission to alter "darker" to "sterner". Do not let us speak of "darker days", let us speak rather of "sterner days". These are not dark days: these are great days – the greatest days our country has ever lived . . .!'

The songs are sentimental and nostalgic, the tunes catching and emotional. Harrovians and Old Harrovians alike come under their spell. There are always so many requests for tickets to 'School Songs' that every seat is taken, and some have to stand at the back of Speech Room. Each year a new boy is chosen to sing solo. It is a daunting prospect.

A favourite solo was 'Five Hundred Faces'. The new boy's virginal voice could be clearly heard throughout the room. The tension was electric. Old Harrovian dignitaries fixed their eyes on the phrase heading this song in the Song Book, *Forsan et haec olim meminisse juvabit*, 'The memory of our griefs and fears may stir the soul in after years', and were unashamed of the tears that rolled down their cheeks in silence:

> *Five hundred faces, and all so strange!*
> *Life in front of me – home behind,*
> *I felt like a waif before the wind*
> *Tossed on an ocean of shock and change.*

We would raise our voices to join in while those in tears blew their noses and mopped their eyes:

> *Yet the time may come, as the years go by,*
> *When your heart will thrill*
> *At the thought of The Hill,*
> *And the day that you came so strange and shy*
> *And the day that you came so strange and shy.*

I too, was enveloped in this sentimental, nostalgic, intoxicating aura, and I watched with sympathy such eminent people as the tall and dignified Nubar Gulbenkian (one of the world's richest men, the son of 'Mr Five Percent'), immaculately dressed, as always, with a large coloured handkerchief at the ready in his breast-pocket, and a magnificent orchid in his buttonhole, picked fresh from his greenhouses. Soon his well-trimmed beard would be soaked with tears, and his beloved wife would press her hand into his to guide him through this taut emotional scene.

After 'Songs', guests were invited to the Head Master's house for refreshments. One year, embarrassed and tongue-tied, I had the task of trying to persuade Nubar Gulbenkian to donate some money to build an indoor swimming-pool. His wife had 'flu at the time, and when I mentioned the swimming-pool, he said gravely, 'Summer colds can be very dangerous.' I was defeated.

On another occasion, I was pregnant, and unable to squeeze into an ordinary dress. I am a hopeless dressmaker, but being determined not to miss 'Songs' I bought some material and cut out my first pattern – it was dreadful. Eventually I pinned up the hem and rushed to Speech Room. Afterwards, in the Head Master's drawing-room, I stood demurely at the back, trying to hide in the crowd so that no one could see the ladders in my stockings caused by the pins. In the distance, I saw Sir Winston Churchill comfortably seated in a large chair by the fireside, a glass of brandy in his left hand, and the inevitable cigar in his right. The television cameras were waiting outside – an unusual event – but perhaps it was an anniversary. The floodlights suddenly flashed on to the french windows leading from the drawing-room to a balcony overlooking the garden. There were shouts for Churchill to appear. He remained seated – oblivious of the commotion, and somnolent from the effect of the brandies he had drunk. I watched for what seemed to be an age. The guests had fallen quiet, wondering what to do. I decided to go over to him, and said:

'The cameras are outside – they are waiting for you.'

He gave me his empty glass, grabbed my arm and murmured: 'Stay with me – I will need you to be beside me.'

I was reduced to kneeling on the floor while he rose from his armchair, using me as his support. Clumsily rising to my feet, I found myself struggling to the window still clinging to the empty brandy glass, and with Churchill clutching my shoulder. I staggered under his weight. We stood alone in the glare of the lights. Churchill mumbled above me, and wafts of cigar smoke drifted across my face.

Later that evening a friend 'phoned:

'Daphne, dear, I have just seen the television. Was that you I saw under Churchill?'

'Yes, it was I.'

'My dear, I really do think that you could have had a better posture – you missed such an opportunity.'

When I arrived at Harrow, I was dismayed to learn of the tradition that a newly-married wife should dine once in each House wearing her wedding-dress. (The same tradition applied in many colleges in Cambridge at the turn of the century.) My friend Jean Leaf, the wife of a master whose family had been connected with Harrow for generations, had married on the same day as I. As befitted a woman who had represented England at fencing, Jean went in her wedding-dress from House to House on the ceremonial round of dinners. She was the last woman ever to do so. Although I refused to put on my wedding-dress, the hem of which was still held up by pins, I did go to dinner in all but one of the Houses. The exception was the House of a bachelor Old Harrovian who refused to invite any member of staff to a meal until they had been at Harrow for three years – and then only if the wife were not pregnant. I did on one occasion get as far as receiving an invitation, which was promptly cancelled when his matron told him that I was three months pregnant. I protested that my pregnancy did not show at all, but he was convinced that my state would in some way be upsetting for the boys – he actually said that there would be no room to move behind my seat at the table.

The boys much preferred their own type of entertaining, which during the fifties consisted of 'finds' breakfast on Sunday mornings. The history of 'finds' went back to the early days, when anyone who had the money to buy a large enough property on The Hill could set up a House and take in boarders. The students paid him for their board, and contracted separately with the school for their education. House servants were paid by the housemaster from his own pocket. On Sunday mornings the servants were given time off to attend a Church service, and as the housemasters were not prepared to provide part-time staff, the boys had to 'find' their own Sunday breakfasts.

In the fifties Harrow still had a fagging system for the senior boys, and it was the fags who cooked and served the 'finds'. The monitors were splendid hosts, and the fags must have had a crash cookery course to cope with the multitude of goodies which were prepared for these great social occasions. It was the nearest one could get to the fashionable male-only clubs in London. There was a thoroughly relaxed atmosphere, with Sunday papers spread on the tables and an air of gracious living.

The boys at Harrow had, and still have, their own rooms which they decorate and furnish themselves. No two rooms are ever alike. Parents were occasionally persuaded to part with antique furniture or Persian carpets from the ancestral home. Other boys purchased directly from such places as Harrods; but the majority went to end-of-term auctions and filled their rooms with well-worn oddments which were perhaps not so beautiful but still practical.

We were often invited to join the monitors for a late 'finds' breakfast on Sundays, being greeted by the Head of House, dressed immaculately in tails and wearing, as a 'blood's priv', the grey waistcoat of the Philathletic Club (the members of this élite society were in a First XI or First XV). The breakfast was laid in his private suite of rooms and the fags stood anxiously at attention ready to serve. We would be given fruit juice; grapefruit, melon or, on some occasions, papaya; steak, mushrooms, bacon, eggs, kidneys, sausages, tomatoes; a choice of beer or coffee; toast and marmalade; fresh fruit – and raspberries in the summer season.

The fags finished off all that was left after we had staggered back to our homes, too full to eat for another twenty-four hours.

'Finds' entertaining by the boys became a little out of hand towards the end of our stay at Harrow, when dinners on Saturday evenings became fashionable and the less sophisticated 'fry-up' of a well-prepared 'finds' breakfast gave way to pheasants and venison sent down from various family shoots and left to hang in the domestic quarters until they were ready for eating. The ultimate was to have a Fortnum & Mason's or Jacksons catering order, when all manner of exotic foods arrived by special delivery. It was an excellent initiation for me and I think that I can now cope with any social situation and feel quite at home. The boys entertained with such casual grace that at the time we never considered this type of entertainment outrageous, although the contrast to our own home environment was ludicrous. I understand that 'finds' dinners do not occur now.

Although our salary was meagre, in term time we lived very well for the boys and their parents were generous with their hospitality. In the holidays we had to rely on my brother-in-law who was a hospital houseman. We would join him for weekend meals. I particularly remember the Royal Masonic Hospital, where the medical staff seemed to live as if in a four-star hotel, dining on game and salmon sent by Masons from all over the country, served with excellent wines. Another friendly provider was the publisher Rupert Hart-Davis, who had accepted John's novel *The Custard Boys*. Rupert used often to invite us to lunch in Soho with Ruth, one of his editors, later to be his wife. I asked:

'Why do you invite us here so often? You sit and watch us eat while you both toy with a salad.'

'It entertains us. It is rare to see any guests appreciate their food as much as you do!' was his immediate reply.

I remember one occasion three years after our marriage when John's aunt and uncle brought us a large ripe pineapple, something John had never seen before. I was thrilled, carefully stood it in a bowl by the window, and made up my mind to produce a meal worthy of this delightful delicacy. As his aunt and uncle departed, John said: 'Thank you very much for the cactus – do we have to put it into some soil?' The following day, I bought the first joint of meat in three years of married life. With pride I selected topside, made the Yorkshire puddings, roasted the potatoes and prepared the vegetables, picked from the school fields and gardens. I laid the table with shining silver and bought black candles for the candelabra. It was a special occasion, and I was suitably dressed in my best evening wear. The moment came when I placed the joint in front of John and handed him the carving knife. He cut the joint down the middle, and handed me my half on a plate.

Come away, O come away
To the splashing and the spray!
Come away, O come away
Ducker is the place today.

Ducker

See the summer sun is glowing,
And the fields are cracked with heat,
Not a breath of air is going
In the hot and dusty street.
This is not a day to swelter,
Toss your book and pen away!
Ducker is the only shelter,
Ducker is the place today.

Until early in the nineteenth century, the boys at Harrow swam in the Old Duck Puddle – it was unhygienic and foul. Then a piece of land was excavated on the other side of the London Road, and a 'New Duck Puddle' became the bathing-area. As unhygienic and foul as the former pool, it was described in Laborde's *Harrow School Yesterday and Today* (1948) as a 'confined pond of stagnant fluid standing on a bed of deep soft ooze, much frequented by water-snakes'. It was Dr Vaughan, Head Master from 1845 to 1860, who from his own pockets first lined the interior of this New Duck Puddle, which, freed from water-snakes, became known as Ducker. Although it was during Vaughan's reign in office that fifth- and sixth-formers founded the Philathletic Club to promote an interest in organised games, he himself was said to have hated games – he was no athlete, but a distinguished scholar – and swimming was the only sport in which he showed any interest.

Ducker must be the envy of many schools. It is fully five hundred feet long and gently curved so that someone standing at one end cannot see the other. Its width varies from sixty to a hundred feet, and when full it holds over 800,000 gallons of water. Not only is it one of the largest swimming-pools in Europe, but it must certainly be one of the most beautiful. There are beds of roses circling the pool, and grass banks on which to lie and sunbathe. Round the circumference mature trees provide shady areas and ensure privacy from the busy London Road.

Today part of Ducker is heated, and boys are now able to swim in comfort for most of the Summer Term. Previously, the temperature of the water had to reach 58° before anyone was allowed to swim.

It was the policy that all boys should be taught to swim and the final stage was to take the Dolphin test. Those who were successful were known as the Dolphins, and had special privileges.

All this was a far cry from my own school days up in Scotland. We had no pool, but we did have the River Tay running freely through our grounds. Our games mistress thought that we were a tough lot, and never used a thermometer to test the temperature of the water. On the first day of the summer term that the sun dared to show its face, we were marched off to our dormitories to collect swimming-costumes and towels. Then we had a 'good bracing run' as we chased after the mistress across the fields, leaping over the fences, to plunge into the icy cold water. It was pointless trying to teach us specific strokes as the water flowed fast, carrying along branches of trees. We swam under water, intruding into sudden, black, deep pools where the fish lurked. The Tay is known for its excellent fishing, and I wonder how much harm we did. On balmy summer nights, we would often make a fire on the stony banks of the river, and while someone boiled soup, the madder members of our year would strip naked and dive for stones. We never knew what the rushing water would bring out of the dark, and were frequently confronted by sheep's carcasses floating past.

They were carefree, giddy days. The current was strong, the water deep, and we were being irresponsible – yet I never heard of anyone getting into difficulties. Exhausted and happy, we would drag ourselves from the river and dry in front of the fire, our bodies tingling with new vitality, then drink our hot soup and return fatigued and exhilarated to our beds, allowing our wet hair to drip on to the pillows.

My love of night-bathing continues to this day. During the

summer months at Harrow, John and I would often creep illegally to the confines of Ducker on the way home from a dinner party, or returning from a hot evening in London, strip off our evening clothes and silently glide through the water with only the moon and the stars to guide us, and the owls to hoot and watch. For ten years we broke the school rules, and during all this time we never met other offenders.

Ducker was looked after by John Campkin who kept the grounds spotless. He and his wife Phyllis ran an excellent tuck-shop with all types of goodies to buy. They lived in Ducker Cottage, which was weatherproof but had no bathroom. I remember them boiling water for their large tin bath. Mrs Campkin seemed to have a constant line of washing suspended in the sun, and she had a special way of drying her woollens, which were hung up by nylon stockings so that the outstretched arms were crucified on the line. Campkin was paid very little money – they had two children to keep, and life was difficult for them, but they were a wonderful couple, always happy and caring.

It was not long before John was asked to be in charge of swimming. He was happy, and looked forward to training the boys. I was startled to find that this involved his being 'on duty' most of the weekends, and that I was not allowed anywhere near the pool as *puris naturalibus* was the rule. I have encountered a vast number of local traditions in my life and have learned that they are not all necessarily good. Nude swimming in Ducker was one example. I tolerated two weekends without seeing John, then decided to write to Dr James pleading my case. Either they had to find another person to run Ducker (and John was the only swimming blue on the staff), or the school would be responsible for a premature separation – or, most sensible of all, the boys could wear swimming-trunks at weekends.

The following day, notices were placed on the two entry doors to the bathing-area stating, in effect, that 'Mrs John Rae wished to accompany her husband at the weekends, and therefore it would be compulsory for boys to wear costumes at this time.'

There was an outcry. Old Harrovians wrote to the Head Master, and letters poured into the editor's letter-box for the school magazine, complaining that the boys would all end up as homosexuals if they were made to cover themselves during the weekends – on weekdays nude bathing was still to be the rule. A chaplain on the staff wrote to John: 'I find that little boys are more erotic with costumes than in the nude' – a remark which said more about the chaplain than about the boys. An Old Harrovian master was so angry that he said he would fight for nudity, nothing would induce him to don a costume. The Head Master did not relent, and neither did I, and with John's encouragement, I accompanied him the following Saturday. We were greeted with enthusiasm from the boys, who had often found nudity embarrassing in modern times. (The swimming team had always had the privilege of wearing trunks.) All went well that day. I was the only wife to brave the area for the first weeks, and I had been warned by the boys that I would find the Old Harrovian master sunbathing in the nude. Sure enough, there he was, the only person left naked – but lying on his stomach, pretending to be asleep. He persevered for another weekend, then realised that he was losing the battle, and that none of the boys had joined him in sympathy. He retired gracefully, and I believe never entered the Ducker precincts again, dressed or not. Soon after this the boys requested that swimming-trunks should be worn throughout the week. I heard that the only other people who were disappointed were students at the local girls' school. A number of them had purchased field-glasses, and found that if they stood on the bridge which the boys used to cross the London Road, they could spend many happy hours. Now the field-glasses were redundant.

My protest had another good effect. The masters' families found the area so congenial that it became a communal meeting-place, and family bathing-times were extended. Mrs Campkin was delighted, as she was able to help her very busy husband by serving in the tuck-shop – previously she had not been able to do very much as she had had to keep out of the way of the nude bathers. The masters' children often swam before they could walk, and the boys were not embarrassed to be seen giving the little ones lessons.

One drawback to family bathing was that at weekends crowds of friends arrived, until Ducker looked like Blackpool Sands. It became difficult for masters and their wives to find excuses to refuse other families entrance. As one master said, 'I never knew that I had so many friends. On the first day of sun, my telephone continually rings, and the voices at the other end all say – "It seems such a long time . . . I thought I would bring the family over to see you".' So now there are subscriptions and passes, and outside school hours Ducker is a club for the élite. But when I last visited the place, there were still no changing-rooms, just open sheds with benches where men and women, children and boys, dress and undress together. Perhaps this may satisfy the objectors who feared that abandoning the nude-bathing tradition would encourage homosexuality.

The picture of public schools as breeding-grounds for homosexuality still exists. They are seen as causing enormous damage to boys' developing sexuality and jeopardising their chances of successful marriages in the future, while masters are regarded as being, in many cases, latent or active homosexuals who may well seduce the young boys in their care.

I have mentioned the nude bathing at Ducker, and the indignation and fear of some people – Old Harrovians to a man – that for the boys to cover themselves would be to open the door to all sorts of vice. (In a way the idea is similar to the old practice in some convent schools of making the girls wear bathing-costumes in their bath in case the angels should be upset by the sight of their nude bodies.) The boys themselves were anxious to wear swimming-trunks, but although George Bernard Shaw said, and rightly, that a woman fully clothed can have more sex appeal than one totally naked, and the Harrow chaplain thought that boys in trunks were more erotic than those without, I doubt whether the bathers had seduction in mind. Even today, modesty exists.

Preventive measures against homosexuality include cold baths, communal bathing (two teams at a time), and removing the lavatory doors. A cold bath may cause a temporary decrease in libido, but nobody can stay in it all day, and there has to be a time when the body warms up again. Communal bathing is supposed to make indecent behaviour impossible. Perhaps it does, but imagine the effect on a potential homosexual of being surrounded by twenty or more healthy male bodies. If you find that difficult, imagine a heterosexual boy bathing with a couple of dozen glamorous, naked females. Sadly for the planners, experience in prisons shows that unless inmates are kept in solitary confinement, two people will always find a way of getting together.

Conditions in schools in earlier times certainly favoured homosexuality. In 1560 Westminster's rules stated that boys must sleep two in a bed. In the late eighteenth and early nineteenth centuries, fifty-two boys shared large beds, 4½ feet wide, in the Long Chamber at Eton, sleeping together 'for sex, or huddled close for warmth'. At Harrow, the scholars slept two or three to a bed until

1805, when Dr Butler became Head Master, and even during his era (1805–29) a special fee was necessary to reserve a boy a bed to himself.

The history of any school of long standing probably includes instances of serious involvements between masters and boys. Nicholas Udall, Head Master of Eton from 1534 to 1543, was said by Walter Haddon to be 'the best schoolmaster and the greatest beater of our time'. His flagrant sexual behaviour with the boys was publicly exposed in 1541. Christopher Hollis describes the scandal in his history of Eton:

'Two Eton boys, Cheney and Hoorde, both of good family, were apprehended in a robbery, in collaboration with the Master's servant, of some silver images and plate from the College. They retorted by accusing Udall of having been in the plot with them and also of having committed sexual offences with them. The whole case was considered so serious that it was investigated by the Privy Council. The Privy Council's verdict was that Udall had not been concerned in the robbery but had been guilty of the sexual offences, to which indeed he confessed. The matter is somewhat obscure but what seems probable is that the boys, caught red-handed in burglary, attempted to blackmail their school-master into doing nothing about it by threatening to reveal his sexual misdemeanours with the boys, which were so notorious that, once revealed, Udall had no hope of exculpating himself.'[5]

An Act of Parliament had recently been passed making the extreme homosexual offence – buggery – a capital offence punishable by death. However, headmasters of public schools are rarely hanged; instead Udall was imprisoned, and after his release he went on to become Head Master of Westminster.

One of the leading Victorian headmasters, the Rev. C. J. Vaughan, Head Master of Harrow from 1845 to 1860, was himself involved in homosexuality. There is no doubt that he was con-sidered a great headmaster. Sir Charles Dalrymple wrote of him that he was the 'Restorer of Harrow'. During his time, discipline became firm, drunkenness was eradicated, and he did much for the religious life of the school – too much, maybe, for one pupil, John Addington Symonds, complained in a letter to his sister Charlotte, on May 17, 1857, 'Do you not think 4 services, 3 ser-mons and 1 school are too much in this hot weather?' However, Symonds's *Memoirs* prove that, sexually speaking, this reformed Harrow of the eighteen-forties and early eighteen-fifties was a jungle. In his biography, *John Addington Symonds* (1964), Grosskurth describes how this sensitive adolescent, from an affectionate and indulgent family, found himself thrust into a brutally lustful society where every good-looking boy was given and addressed by a female name and was either 'public property' or owned by an older boy whose 'bitch' he became. Symonds particularly remembered the treatment of one sensual-mouthed boy whose lovers, among them several monitors, turned against him: they used him savagely in public, kicked him, spat at him, and threw books at him until he ran away in terror.

Vaughan made great efforts to put a stop to homosexuality at Harrow, but unfortunately he himself had an affair with a lively good-looking boy, Alfred Pretor, who showed Symonds some of the passionate letters the Head Master had sent him. Symonds was profoundly shocked and troubled. One day he had to take an essay to Vaughan's study and was sitting beside the Head Master on a sofa when Vaughan began gently to stroke his thigh. Symonds trembled with agitation, remembering Pretor's revelations. Eventually, after he had gone up to Oxford, Symonds told his father about the Head Master's relationship with Pretor. Dr Symonds, an Associate of the Royal College of Physicians, was outraged and forced Vaughan to resign. Mrs Vaughan, a kind, gentle and much-respected woman, pleaded with Dr Symonds on her husband's behalf. She knew his weakness, but insisted that it had never interfered with his service to Harrow. Dr Symonds was moved by her plea but would not change his mind. A few months later, when Vaughan was offered the bishopric of Rochester, Dr Symonds made him refuse it. In 1879, after Dr Symonds's death, Vaughan became Dean of Llandaff.

The situation today is not as blatant, but there is no doubt that homosexual activity goes on. An Augustinian nun is quoted as saying of the sexual instinct: 'You can't sublimate it, you can't suppress it, you simply have to damn well sacrifice it.' Sublimation seems to be nearly impossible. Kinsey reported in 1948 that in a sample of nearly 13,000, he had found 'not a single clear-cut example'. It is impossible to judge just how much physical sexuality occurs in contemporary single-sex public schools, but one estimate is that about twenty-five per cent of boys between thirteen and eighteen will have a homosexual experience leading to orgasm. Concealment and secrecy often prevail, as the following story shows.

At a well-known and highly-respected public school, a Head of

82

House was recently discovered to be using his authority to force younger boys to indulge in homosexual activity with him. The father of one of the younger boys heard of this and was determined that something should be done. The housemaster refused to believe him so he approached the Head of House's father. The latter was one of the most powerful men in the City and he made it clear that if the boy's father did not drop the enquiry at once, he would personally see that his career was destroyed. Undeterred, the boy's father approached the new headmaster, who was sufficiently worried to set up an internal inquiry. Unfortunately he put it in the hands of a retired housemaster, himself an Old Boy of the school, of all men the least likely to find anything wrong with the school to which he had devoted his life. As was to be expected, the inquiry concluded that there was no case to answer. The boy's father then turned to the Governors. They took the line that the headmaster had looked into the matter and there was nothing more to be done. However, one Governor was suspicious. Instead of letting the matter rest, he decided to make enquiries himself. As a result, the true story was exposed. The housemaster was immediately sacked, but the corrupt Head of House was merely demoted – the reason given being that he had been promoted too young. The son used his power to corrupt younger boys: the father used his power to protect his son: it is an archetypical public-school and Establishment story.

There is another type of homosexual relationship which must also be considered: the highly emotional, idealised and idealistic love which can exist between two boys (or two girls), usually, though not invariably, of considerably different ages. The younger partner in such a relationship is often a very 'pretty' boy with feminine features and an unbroken voice. The older partner's feelings can thus be seen as part of his developing sexuality, and with no particular homosexual bias. The rivalry that frequently exists between several older boys for the affections of a younger one is exactly comparable to the competition between adult males for a particular female.

In 1807 at the age of nineteen, whilst an undergraduate at Trinity College, Cambridge, Byron wrote to Elizabeth Pigot expressing his feelings for a choirboy, John Edleston, to whom he had written a poem, *The Cornelian*, and who was 'exactly to an hour 2 years younger than myself':

'I rejoice to hear you are interested in my protégé, he has been my *almost constant* associate since October 1805 when I entered Trinity College . . . his *voice* first attracted my notice, his *countenance* fixed it, and his *manner* attached me to him forever. . . . I certainly *love* him more than any human being, & neither *time* or Distance have had the least effect on my (in general) changeable Disposition.'[3]

Some years earlier, in 1803, Byron had had an unfortunate experience in the role of the younger boy in such a relationship. Baron Grey de Ruthyn, a young man of twenty-three, invited him to stay, and apparently made some aberrant sexual advances to the boy, which offended and revolted him. He wrote to his half-sister Augusta on March 26, 1804, saying that he was not reconciled to Lord Grey ('He was once my *Greatest Friend*') and never would be. This experience caused Byron much unhappiness, for he wrote to Augusta again on October 25, 1804, from Harrow School, saying:

'I feel a little inclined to laugh at you, for love in my humble opinion is utter nonsense, a mere jargon of compliments, romance, and deceit; now for my part had I fifty mistresses, I should in the course of a fortnight forget them all, and if by any chance I ever recollected one, should laugh at it as a dream, and bless my stars for delivering me from the hands of the little mischievous Blind God.'[3]

Idealised emotional experiences can be very profound, and in them the physical side may play little or no part. Byron's affair with Lord Grey is one instance where the whole relationship was ruined by becoming physical. The language of love is used, notes and glances are exchanged, and there is a very high degree of mutual caring. While most of these experiences are transient, some may develop into life-long friendships of great value. It is therefore unwise, and possibly dangerous, to try to isolate homosexual episodes from an adolescent's developing sexuality – dangerous because repressive measures may well damage his ability to make meaningful relationships in later life. Similarly, a homosexual master, who may find it difficult to experience a happy sexual relationship in marriage, may be able to generalise his feelings to include many, or all, of the boys with whom he comes in contact. Such a master can be an asset to the school, particularly where there are young, sensitive boys who feel lost away from home.

Public-school masters, even without any personal homosexual inclination, tend to play down the existence of homosexuality and even delude themselves into believing that it does not happen.

When a headmaster retired recently, he was quoted by the Press as saying that homosexuality was not a problem in his school. I am reminded of a conference between headmasters and the police on drug-taking. One headmaster stated categorically that there were no drug-users at his school. A policewoman from the Drug Squad who had said nothing till that point told him: 'Headmaster, I could give you the names of three of your present pupils who have used heroin, and a dozen more who regularly smoke pot.' There seems to be no doubt that homosexual experiences, both physical and emotional, do occur in public schools – though not in every school, to every boy, at every time. Sometimes two or three boys 'start a fashion' and this may spread to involve most of the school.

An Old Harrovian who left 'under a cloud' in the nineteen-fifties recently sent me a description of his last summer term which set his own experiences of school relationships vividly in context. He was seventeen and had been at Harrow three years. As a 'three-yearer' he had certain privileges, such as the right to have a wire-less in his room, or to wear a white scarf. Above him in the school hierarchy came the 'four-yearers', and above them the House monitors. His housemaster got on well with 'House-spirited' boys, who enjoyed going sailing and having a beer with him; the boy and his friends were not of this type. That summer his best friend fell ill and was sent to the San, and he was left to drift about the House ('claustrophobic and hierarchical'). He remembers it as a time of hanging around, taking little interest in school, lounging at the cricket fields, blowing Benson & Hedges up the chimney, and thinking of London. He fell briefly for a beautiful fourteen-year-old boy. Then came a more serious relationship:

'One of the school heroes and I became attracted to each other. Both from the same House. A civilised House.

An angry retort flew from my lips at one of our four-yearers in the fives court. Reported for "lip", summoned to Reader [the House library], beaten by the Head of House. My three-year privileges taken away.

A last few weeks of reckless affection with my god-like friend. Some drink I think. My House beak sent me to the Head Master. I met him for the first time. He was surprised I wanted to leave.'[6]

The question is, whether experiences such as this do any harm to the boys. Public schools do not *create* homosexuals. Dr Ismond Rosen states it clearly in his book *Sexual Deviation*:

'Sexual orientation is settled at a very early age. There is now a con-siderable body of evidence to suggest that the most important factor bearing on the acquisition of gender role – that is, whether a person feels himself to be male or female – is the sex that the child is assigned to by his parents and thus the sex in which he is brought up . . . such data suggests that sex-role identity is becoming well established by the age of three years. Sex differences in children's behaviour and attitudes are also evident from early childhood and quite marked at the age of four to five years, although differences continue to increase up to eight or nine years.'[7]

Every parent and schoolmaster knows that adolescence is a turbulent time as teenagers become increasingly aware of the drives within them. While they search for a personal identity, so they realise, consciously or unconsciously, that they can only become a whole person through a relationship with another. Becoming whole in this way does not necessarily involve physical expression, but sudden violent increases in sexual awareness and potency mean that it will very likely do so. By the time he leaves school every boy will probably have had a sexual experience, whether hetero- or homosexual, or by masturbation. The public school with its enforced monasticism merely reduces the chances of a heterosexual experience, and may delay its development. The majority of boys – their orientation settled long before entry to school – eventually go on to make perfectly normal heterosexual relationships. The homosexual minority may be saved from adult unhappiness and disastrous marriages by an early recognition of their true sexual identity.

Once again, it is all too easy to concentrate – mistakenly – on the physical aspect. The assumption that sexual experiences in adolescence are rather like acne – almost inevitable and rather unpleasant – ignores the linking of sexual experience with love. Dr Jack Dominian, a psychiatrist with a long experience of dealing with marital problems, remarked to a correspondent (1980), 'The greater the love which exists in a relationship, the more appropriate is the presence of sex . . . sex and love belong to one another.' He sees sex as 'sealing a relationship that has developed on a basis of complementarity', not for 'exploration of human relationships', and still less as 'experimentation in which people are treated as objects'. Adult society today – with 'girlie' magazines, pornographic films, live sex shows and the like – does its best to separate the two, and then moralises over the increasing divorce rate. Children and adolescents need to be educated in the positive relationship between love and sex if they are to have any real hope of making successful marriages.

86

I gave this manuscript to a peer and his son. Interested by my views on relationships between staff and pupils, they told me a story. The son, now in the regular Army, said that all but three members of his year at a well-known public school had been taught the various pleasures of sexual activity by the young and beautiful wife of a master. 'She was a quite extraordinary woman, and it was common knowledge amongst the boys that this experience was available. She would concentrate on a year at a time – there were about a hundred of us in my year, all aged about sixteen.' I asked about the three boys who were left out of these erotic practices. 'They hadn't the courage to go through with it,' he replied. 'I met one of them recently and he said he had missed a golden opportunity.' I am not sure how the Head Master found out, but the husband was asked to leave and recommended to try another profession. The wife was so distraught that the couple parted company – 'I cannot live without my young boys around me.' I wonder if she applied for a job as matron! What surprised me was that both son and father accepted the situation – admittedly with a laugh – they took the Victorian line that it could do no harm for those young men to be given the extra education free of charge – presumably it would save the expense of an *affaire de coeur Parisienne*.

The implication behind the criticism of public schools as causing homosexuality (which they do not in fact do) is that homosexuality is not good for society. The real situation, however, is not nearly as simple. A protective, idealistic, loving relationship between two adolescents may well serve as a model for future relationships, including marriage, and furnish an incentive to make them succeed. We have moved in our judgment of homosexuality from thinking of it as nothing more than a furtive act in public lavatories, to realising that at its highest it is a sensitive and beautiful relationship – and one which can give a great deal to the world, particularly through the creative arts. We are all quite prepared to make the obvious distinction between an ideal marriage and a casual encounter with a prostitute; surely we can apply the same distinction to homosexual relationships? Nor is the physical side of such a relationship straightforward. R. V. Sherwin in his book *Sexual Behaviour and the Law* (1965) has pointed out that orgastic pleasure may be insignificant; the mutual dependency of homosexuals, which is often intense, 'may be far more important than sexual activity'.

Any school must safeguard younger boys against seduction by the older ones, and be vigilant against rape – whether the proferred violence be physical or mental. But this is true of all sexual relationships, hetero- or homosexual. It is an extension of the principle that the young must not be subjected to any violent experience with which they cannot cope, because they cannot assimilate it into their own frame of experience.

Bullying is, of course, sadism under another name, another expression of increasing sexuality taking the wrong turning. One master recently told me that he could match every eighteenth-century story of bullying in schools with one from the last ten years. It reaches its peak in boarding-schools, partly because boys are together for such long periods of time, and the victim is unable to escape, but partly too, because of the absence of girls and the impossibility of normal sexual expression – even if only in fantasy. Girls and boys grow up more normally together than apart. Public schools are introducing mixed-sex sixth forms, but the need is not confined to the adolescent years; it is there throughout school life. Some schools have recognised this, and admit girls at an earlier age. 'Since girls joined the sixth form in 1970,' one headmaster said, 'the boys have become gentler.'

What about religious attitudes? Modern knowledge of the genetic, hormonal and psychological factors affecting gender must eliminate any idea of homosexual orientation as morally wrong. It is not for me to judge what two adults answerable to their own consciences, do in the privacy of their own lives, particularly when I have no knowledge of the pressures under which they live.

Chapel

The history of worship at Harrow School goes back to 1591, when the founder John Lyon drew up what is referred to as his last Will – a document entitled *Orders, Statutes and Rules*. In the appendix he gave detailed instructions as to the religious education of the boys, and the number of church attendances to be enforced. On Sundays, all boys had to attend the parish church, St Mary's, a beautiful building situated on the highest point of The Hill. It was here that the preacher was paid the vast sum of six shillings and eight pence for each of thirty 'good, learned and godly sermons'. The resulting payment of £10 per year compares with the annual payment of £26 14s. 4d. for a master provided by John Lyon's will.

St Mary's continued to be the place of worship for Harrovians for nearly 250 years. The headmastership of the disciplinarian Dr George Butler, 1805 to 1829, was notable in that two of his pupils later became staunch supporters of the Roman Catholic Church. One was Frederick William Faber, received into the Church in 1845: he founded London's Brompton Oratory nine years later. The other, Henry Manning, who was sent to Harrow in 1822, was to become Cardinal Archbishop of Westminster, a contemporary of Cardinal Newman, and a friend of Prime Minister Gladstone. Mr Richmond, the artist, wrote: 'In his Harrow days, Manning was a "buck" of the first water, as dandies or "heavy swells" were then called. Among other adornments, he sported Hessian top-boots with tassels, rather an extreme piece of foppery in a Harrow boy.' Manning himself recalled his Harrow schooldays in his journal:

'We were literally without religious guidance or formation. The services in the church were for most of the boys worse than useless . . . Harrow was certainly the least religious time of my life: I had faith, a great fear of Hell, and said my prayers; beyond, all was blank . . . Butler used to walk up and down in the Great School and call upon us to read. I only remember one thing that he once said, but it did me good, that when we were laughed at for religion, angels were rejoicing over us . . . Harrow was a pleasant place and my life there was a pleasant time, but I look back on it with sadness.'[8]

C. R. Nevinson describes his days at Uppingham some eighty years later in similar terms:

'I attended divine services; listened to strange sermons delivered by Doctors of Divinity, in which Englishmen were confused with God, Nelson with Jesus Christ, Lady Hamilton with the Virgin Mary. The German Fascists . . . are fed on no greater confusion of patriotism and religion.'[2]

George Butler's successor, Charles Thomas Longley (1829–36), was an undistinguished Head Master, and though he later became, in 1862, Archbishop of Canterbury, he made no lasting contribution to the school's religious life. He was followed by Christopher Wordsworth, appointed Head Master in 1836. Although during his reign in office the number of students fell to sixty-nine, Christopher Wordsworth had one great achievement to his credit. He persuaded the Governors to build a small School Chapel in 1839, at a cost of £3,847 12s. 9d. It was consecrated by the Archbishop of Canterbury, Dr William Howley.

In Wordsworth's era the discipline of the school was poor. He felt that, through the pulpit, he could awaken the Christian spirit and restore discipline. Unfortunately he was not successful. As a boy he had achieved a brilliant academic career at Winchester. In *Athleticism in the Victorian and Edwardian Public School* (1981), J. A. Mangan wrote that he had 'that blend of intellectualism, piety and physical talent so common to nineteenth-century muscular Christians'. His outstanding excellence in all the major sports won him the title of 'the Great Christopher'. Had he spoken from the pulpit of the glory of the playing-fields, had he drawn comparisons between athletic prowess and the task of building the British Empire, he might have won his listeners' allegiance because of his own achievements. But he did not. Perhaps he was too modest. In a period notable for the publishing of volumes of sermons, ambitious headmasters were quick to get into print with what Mangan calls their 'moral clichés and high-minded exhortations', 'their personal idealism and educational philosophy', thus displaying to the public the tone of their school and the calibre of their headmastership. Wordsworth's humility stood against his becoming a great headmaster in those undisciplined days.

Under Wordsworth's successor, Charles John Vaughan (1845–60), 'the Restorer of Harrow', the number of boys swiftly increased, and soon the Chapel proved too small. Vaughan was a wealthy man and, again from his own pockets, he financed an extension costing over £2,500 – a generous sum of money in 1854. Many other improvements and extensions have followed, up to the present time.

During our years at Harrow, there was a rule that apart from masters and boys, 'none but Old Harrovians, parents of boys, and strangers introduced by a master can attend the Chapel services, except at special invitation of the Head Master'. From the time of the earliest building, special pews were provided for masters' wives and friends of the school. In 1955, when I first arrived at Harrow, the pews in the ladies' transept, known as the 'hen-coop', were situated to the south-east of the altar. There was a strict code of conduct amongst the wives. The Head Master's wife and the senior housemasters' wives sat in the front row, and the junior members sat in the back rows. Hats were worn. I did not possess a hat and as no senior wife reprimanded me, I saw no need to buy one (by the time we left, in the mid-sixties, it was rare for any wife to cover her head).

Soon after our arrival, the wives requested a change of seating as they felt conspicuous sitting in front of the boys. This was agreed. Instead of the transept pews, five back rows in the nave were reserved for masters' families. I missed the first two services that followed the move, and when I arrived one Sunday evening, three weeks later, I slipped into the back row, which I took to be the most junior position. The service was due to begin. The Head Master's wife, Bobbie James, came and knelt beside me. Whilst I was still praying, a wife sitting in the row in front of me handed me a note. 'You are sitting in the most senior pew – only for the use of the wives of the senior housemasters – you should be sitting in the front few rows.' It was signed by a senior wife. I looked up and found Custos (the Head Porter) standing in the aisle at the end of my pew, beckoning me to come out.

'I'm afraid you can't sit there, Mrs Rae,' said Custos, 'I'm sorry, but I was asked to tell you.' He looked very upset and embarrassed.

Amazed and angry that such pettiness could exist in what was meant to be a Christian foundation – particularly as there were plenty of spare seats in the senior rows – I made my way to the aisle, turned on my heel, and walked away as the service started.

Bobbie James had seen me leave the Chapel (I had had to step behind her whilst she was praying), but she had missed the commotion before. However, Custos spoke to her after the service and told her the reason. She wrote a note to me immediately, apologising on behalf of the senior members, and asked me to go and have coffee with her.

Bobbie James was an excellent headmaster's wife – highly intelligent and devoted to her husband; to me they were the ideal married couple. She was always polite, tactful, considerate and sympathetic, and I found that she had a great understanding of the problems of junior wives, whilst at the same time respecting our privacy. I greatly admired her, and failed hopelessly to live up to her standards in later years. I will always remember that first time when we were alone together. She talked to me as an equal about the problems which existed in community living, and after we had had a laugh she said: 'Next Sunday I want you to come in with me and we will sit together.'

I soon learned that Bobbie James had a great gift for organisation. She ran her household skilfully and well with the aid of *au pair* girls, each of whom usually came for one year, and on leaving recommended a friend to follow on. 'We were treated as part of the family,' one girl told me, 'but we had to abide by the rules which Mrs James laid down. We were not allowed out of the house when the boys had their free time, and although we could attend non-official dinner parties, we could never mix with the monitors when they came to dinner – we had to serve them at table.' She was thrilled when she sat near the Archbishop of Canterbury one lunch-time: 'I wrote home to Denmark and told my family about this great honour.' Although the *au pairs* were under such strict discipline, which I am sure was not abused, I know of at least one who married a master, and another who married an Old Boy of the school.

At the beginning of each term, Bobbie James would arrange a wives' tea party. The *au pairs* served delicately-cut, crustless sandwiches, and Indian and China tea, with milk or lemon. There would be glorious cream cakes and biscuits baked by the staff –

Bobbie James maintained that she would have plenty of time to learn to cook in her retirement and that there was no need for her to attempt it in the Head Master's house.

The tea party was a 'welcome back to school' occasion which was accepted and enjoyed. Dr Jimmy James – perhaps under pressure – joined the ladies for tea in the dining-room, but retired when we went into the large black-carpeted drawing-room where there were rows of chairs set out as if for an official meeting – which indeed it was. Psychologically, it was a brilliantly-planned event with good food and friendly company followed by solemn conference. Bobbie took the chair. Every area in which wives could and should participate in the coming term was planned to the last detail. News was given of forthcoming events in the Middlesex area. Contacts were arranged with those living on The Hill who were anxious to be included in the school community. A list to be signed by volunteers willing to provide and arrange the flowers for Chapel was handed round. I was always glad to see one particular senior wife, Audrey Malan, sign her name each time. Her arrangements would delight any artist. In her youth she had travelled unaccompanied to the Far East, an unheard-of achievement for any young woman in those days, and wrote an account of her travels. Was it her sense of exploration which gave her the ability to transform lettuce leaves and stalks of rhubarb, together with more conventionally decorative vegetation, into works of art?

After the notices for the term had been read out, there was the usual 'Any other business' – a time when we could suggest future schemes, and thus become involved at a deeper level and express our own opinions. I remember our talking of forming a volunteer group for the Samaritans, and discussing donations of money to a variety of charitable organisations. We left the official tea party under the impression – and rightly so – that we were an important part of the school community, and through this, we became increasingly proud to belong to Harrow.

Without these tea parties, I am certain that there would have been far more gossip among the wives. Bobbie James's meetings convinced me how important it is to any school that the wives should all meet once a term.

It was also Bobbie who organised what John called 'The Goodly Wives Committee' – a group of people living near the school, but not necessarily connected with it, who would volunteer family help in an emergency. They were, I believe, devoted and kind (sometimes over-kind according to a district nurse who told me of an alcoholic 'squatting' on school property, whose room was cleaned daily and whose meals were prepared while he lay undisturbed in a drunken stupor, suffering from the 'night before'; he had never had it so good, and decided to stay a squatter). The only experience that my family had of the Goodly Wives was when I fell ill. I had had a sleepless night, and felt very sick at the thought of food. John took it casually, and said that he felt sick too. My first thought was that my cooking was at fault. I urged John out of bed, breakfasted him, and sent him to school groaning. Then I telephoned my doctor, and asked her to call on her rounds. When she arrived, I felt fine, and greeted her jovially. 'You must go straight into hospital,' she said to my amazement. 'You have appendicitis – I can smell it on your breath.'

I was extremely indignant at the thought that my breath smelt, and telephoned John telling him to return and remove this mad woman! (She was a good friend, and I seriously believed that she was joking.) John returned, still groaning with pain, and I said with glee, 'Oh, the smell is John's.' I refused to go to the hospital, John retired to bed with a hot-water bottle, and my doctor telephoned the surgeon to come and convince me of my medical predicament. As soon as the surgeon stepped into the house, he said: 'Yes, you must come immediately, or it will be too late.'

'Nonsense – it's my husband's smell, not mine,' I answered feebly, and directed him into the bedroom where John was lying gasping on the bed. The surgeon whipped the slumberdown off him, and said: 'For heaven's sake get up, and put some sense into your wife's head, she must return with me.'

Without even examining me, they swept me off to hospital, removed my appendix, and told me I was lucky not to leave the theatre in a wooden coat. I have been very aware of breath smells since that day.

In the meantime, the 'goodly works ladies' arrived to help cope with the children, which was easy, and with John, who was impossible. He made them so nervous that they had to leave the house as soon as he entered it – but they brought food, which was left in the oven, and they were kind. I was still in hospital, my stitches not yet removed, when I received a 'phone call from John: 'I told the goodly wives that I was picking you up today, and not to come back.' Four and a half days after the operation I was to be found painfully wheeling a trolley round Sainsbury's while John sat in our drawing-room watching an international rugger match. His first priority.

In our latter years at Harrow, Bobbie James decided that a fortnightly newsletter would help to keep us all in touch during term. This was a tremendous feat. Requests for help, news items and announcements were sent directly to her: she had to sort them all out and rewrite them in letter form. This she typed herself, made photostat copies, and delivered them to the wives. She made it seem easy, but it involved an immense amount of work.

That first time Bobbie James and I talked alone together after the Chapel contretemps, she remarked how important it was to have outside interests. I was then working at a local home for unmarried mothers and she asked a great many questions about it. Harrow recognised the importance of social work, and the school ran a boys' club in Paddington, to which John and I used to go each week – he was in charge of it for some years – with a few of the boys who wanted to help. The club was supposed to be for the poor and destitute. Housing in that area was certainly disgraceful. Frequently there was no running water, and several families had to share a lavatory which was inevitably blocked. However, when I arrived at the club on my first evening, I had an energetic game of table tennis with one of the Paddington boys, and then asked for a coffee at the refreshment bar. My opponent insisted on paying for me: 'I earn a much better salary than your old man. I'm self-employed, can work when I want, where I want, and even make more or less what I want in hard cash – I'm on the barrows.'

This was typical of the people at the club. I remember a camping holiday on the Isle of Wight with a mixture of boys from the club and the school. My young daughter was three months old. The boys put up a drying-line for me, kept me constantly supplied with boiling water for washing nappies, and gave me privacy when I breast-fed the babe. In the evenings they introduced us to the various pubs on the island, and it was always they who insisted on carrying the carry-cot with my delighted child happily inside. After a drive they always offered us petrol money.

The club building was old-fashioned and rather dirty; 'just feels natural', we were told. Further up the road was a second club, run by another school. In an attempt to lure more people it was closed for redecoration. When it was re-opened a few weeks later, it was spotless and practically empty. There were some grand leather chairs, top-quality snooker and billiard tables, bright furnishings and fitted carpets. By the end of the first meeting, there was nearly total destruction. It is all very well for the rich to be rich, but they should not force their wealth so blatantly on others. A lesson was learnt in good manners.

Involving the boys with the needy should always be part of the Chaplain's work. Young men and women in schools such as Harrow often have no idea how the very poor live. They see 'meths' drinkers at a distance, but don't ask why they become addicted. They see alcoholics, drug addicts, beggars, the mentally deranged – but don't look beyond the problem to an environmental cause. A few nights working with the Simon Community or helping with one of the mobile soup kitchens organised by Religious of all denominations, by Humanists, or by people of simple goodwill, may reveal far more than any lecture and bring them to realise that although funds are necessary, giving money to satisfy their consciences is not enough – they must give themselves too. Boys should be encouraged to help prisoners, the physically handicapped, the mentally handicapped, the unloved and lonely in all walks of life. The affluent are often the most lonely, for once they are involved with others who are in need, then loneliness disappears.

The role of chaplain can never have been an easy one. Even in the Victorian era, when compulsory Chapel attendance was taken for granted and schoolmasters were often 'in orders' (in 1866 nine out of the twenty assistant masters at Harrow were ordained), it was a rare preacher who could breathe life into his sermons. As Arnold Lunn (Harrow, 1902–07) was to say:

'My old school is much perturbed by our failure to beat Eton since the War. If Eton won next year's match as the result of a Harrovian, whom we will call Tompkins, dropping a catch just before Eton scored the winning hit, Harrow would go into mourning and Tompkins would never be able to hold up his head again. But if Tompkins dropped his faith, who would care? Yet, if we took Christianity seriously, there would be far more concern amongst the staff if Tompkins lost his faith than if Tompkins lost the match. Nobody bothers much about Tompkins' faith provided that Tompkins is not so ill-bred as to advertise his agnosticism . . . it does not matter what a man believes, provided that he behaves himself.

I never heard while I was at Harrow a single sermon arguing that specifically Christian virtue, the virtue of humility, and yet the gaily bedizened waistcoats of our school bloods would have provided an admirable theme for such a sermon. Athletic swagger is harmless enough – I prefer it to intellectual conceit – but there is no reason why an occasional sermon should not be devoted to convincing the boys that skill in hitting a round ball does not justify a boy assuming that he is a person of outstanding distinction. And yet in my day, no school preacher had the courage to attack that most characteristic of public-school feelings, complacent self-satisfaction and pride of caste.

If Tompkins is a Roman Catholic and ceases to attend Mass the fact is at once noticed, and every effort is made to reclaim him . . . what Roman Catholics have done, Anglicans should be able to do, but to produce the same results involves nothing less than a revolution in our present methods. The trouble is that the schools are not free agents – like other institutions, they depend to some extent on the law of supply and demand. If the school curriculum was altered and if Christianity was taught at the expense of some other subjects with money-making potentialities there might be a fine outcry among parents. Schools cannot supply articles for which there is no public demand. Their job is to train boys for the battle of life – this life.'9

Sunday attendance at Chapel is generally still compulsory, but it is usual for boys to have a choice between a number of different services. After all, it is a rare person indeed who can successfully hold a congregation let alone one ranging in age from twelve to nineteen. Sixth-formers frequently have the option of attending a lecture with prayers.

In Roman Catholic schools, boys may have a choice between High Mass and Low Mass, besides attending optional lectures by visiting speakers, at which questions may be asked and a new depth of Christian understanding achieved.

It takes a special person to be a good and effective chaplain at a boys' public school. What are the ideal qualifications? When John had to appoint a boarding-school chaplain, he decided to advertise in the *Times Educational Supplement*. The postman staggered up the school drive, weighed down with applications. Twenty or so applicants were chosen, and their respective referees, mostly bishops, sent glowing reports on all of them. John was thrilled – but quickly became utterly despondent after the interviews. 'They're all "yes men",' he said, 'every time I ask a question, the answer is "I will do whatever you wish".' He re-read their references and wondered whether the bishops realised whom they were writing about. Later I met one of the referees and asked him why he had written so many glowing reports on men who did not match up to their descriptions. The answer was quick and to the point: 'Well, what would you do if you wanted to get rid of someone from your diocese?'

The Chaplain must be trusted; he must be one of the Head Master's righthand men – and yet the students must be confident that he is not the Head Master's informer. If he is married, his wife will need the patience of a saint. He must be available at all times, day or night. He is the channel of God's love, and through him, God is seen by his fellow masters, as well as by the boys and girls in the school. He must care for and love each person individually – the strong and the weak, the academic and the slow learner, the heterosexual and the homosexual. He must help and love the bully and the thief. There can be no favouritism. He must love until it hurts. Lonely as his position is, he will have the certain knowledge of God's love.

Secure in his own beliefs, a chaplain has also to make allowances for those who belong to other branches of the Christian faith. I was sad when a renowned Anglican canon recently wrote and distributed a paper ridiculing the Roman Catholic belief in the sacrament of the Mass as the Bread of Life – a belief which must never be derided. A good school chaplain will ensure that Roman Catholic pupils have access to the sacraments; he will encourage and support Christian Scientists and members of other minority groups; and his loving care will extend to Jewish and Oriental pupils.

When we were at Harrow, I noticed that there were very few Jewish boys at the school. I thought this was a great misfortune. My daughters went for a time to the North London Collegiate School, where there were a large number of Jewish girls, whose parents were very involved with their children's education. They set an excellent example of family integration and proved a great academic stimulus to my children. I used to wonder why Harrow, so close to the Jewish strongholds in North London, was apparently ostracised by the Jewish community; and only recently found the reason for Harrow's loss. A clause in the Rules stated that if a housemaster decided to accept a Jewish boy – and it was 'a condition of his tenure' to take 'such a boy' from time to time – he must first check with the Head Master, as there must not be more than twenty-five Jews in the school at any one time. This regulation was in force during our period at Harrow, and appeared in the School Rules until at least 1966. The authorities provided a special class for Jewish students on Sunday morning and evening, but no mention was made of Saturday worship. Roman Catholics and Christian Scientists were few in number at Harrow, but there was no official limitation, and they were able to attend their own services. Housemasters had also to be prepared to receive, if necessary, boys of Oriental birth, though no religious instruction was organised for members of Oriental faiths.

During our early years at Harrow, Philip Bryant was the senior School Chaplain. He was a spiritual man and greatly loved by those who knew him well. I used to go to his early-morning Communion services, held on Wednesdays in the Crypt Chapel. Why are such places so bleak and dreary? Yet Philip was able to make the small gathering of a dozen or so boys feel as one. He was always available to the students, and would take any boy back to his study to talk things over. He was particularly helpful and patient with the agnostics on the staff – my husband found him a wise counsellor in this respect. When he died suddenly in 1961, I happened to be in charge of Chapel flowers for his funeral service. Philip had loved flowers, and people gave generously from their own gardens flowers which they arranged themselves. There were vases on every available surface and even the aisles became ablaze with colour – it was a flower festival.

St Augustine said that there are two major sins. If I place myself in a position which could cause hurt to others, I have sinned. If I know something should be done and I fail to acknowledge or do it, then too I have sinned, just as deeply. We can only fully understand these two major sins – which are accepted as such by all major religions – once we are aware of the problems of those around us.

A good school chaplain accepts that he must be available at all times, not only to the boys, but also to the masters. He has to gain their respect, try to understand their foibles and jealousies, be aware of the pettiness and bitterness which can creep into a common room, particularly during the end of a busy term when the weather is poor and the staff are tired. Public-school masters are not a race apart; they may be mature in their teaching, and yet immature in facing the problems of life. They have many psychological involvements, academic as well as emotional. I well remember a senior school inspector saying to me: 'If you decide to send your children to boarding-school, choose a school close to a city or large town, for when the staff become too tense they can escape to a film, play or concert.'

The answer to an 'ideal' school chaplain was exemplified for me by a happy young Benedictine monk who was one of my fellow students at Heythrop Theological College. He was not only outstandingly good-looking, but had obtained a first-class Honours degree at Oxford. Most of the post-graduates on the course were ordained or belonged to religious Orders. When a Jesuit lecturer asked his listeners what had persuaded them to become priests or Religious, there was a long deathly silence. Then Christopher spoke:

'When I was up at Oxford, I fell in love with many lovely girls and couldn't decide which one to marry. I was in a dilemma until I realised that they were all wonderful people, and that people in general really are wonderful – but often shy – and I wanted to love all people. What better way is there than becoming a Religious?'

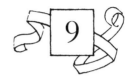

Setting Up Home

I believe that all the staff at Harrow lived on The Hill, and apart from one family who owned a very beautiful house by St Mary's church, I think I am correct in saying that Harrow provided all the accommodation. This was a great asset to a young married couple with no financial backing, but a worry for those who saw their retirement looming up ahead and realised that there was precious little left in the bank to cope with inflation.

Housing is a sensitive subject among married masters. Some of the houses at Harrow were peaceful, beautiful and dry – others were noisy, cold and damp. Some had large gardens – others had virtually none. There were no new houses, and in the nineteen-fifties central heating was unheard of.

When a house became free, due to a master's retiring, or becoming a housemaster, or leaving for a headmastership elsewhere, it was advertised in the Masters' Common Room. Those interested would write to the Head Master, and wait in anticipation and fear that a more senior man might wish to live there.

Our own accommodation at Harrow ranged from Sanatorium Lodge, condemned since 1933, to Peterborough Cottage, which was a most beautiful and perfect flat with views across farmland to London.

Our first possessions consisted of a double bed, a second-hand leather sofa from Harrods, a cooker and a 'fridge. I made curtains from old material found in a disused cupboard in one of the two bedrooms, which opened off the sitting-room. There was no bathroom, but in the corridor which I used as a kitchen stood a cracked tap-less bath, connected to nothing, over which was placed an old door with peeling paint. This became my kitchen table. A dirt-ingrained stone sink stood in one corner, and above it was an ancient gas water-heater which provided an excellent supply of hot water, to a background of explosions and groans. I learnt to hate the sight of dirty pots. The draining-board had always to be cleared of soiled dishes before I felt able to wash my teeth and spit into the sink – there was nowhere else. Later, when our children were born and I had to wash dirty nappies, I used disinfectant liberally.

Apart from a larder and an outside toilet, that was all there was. We moved into Sanatorium Lodge in January, 1956. The weather was bleak and damp. The larder grew mould overnight and the paraffin heater belched out black fumes. The outside toilet was a penance. I would repress nature until I was ready to burst, then clutching a hot-water bottle to my stomach, I would sit on the lavatory seat, tense and waiting to thaw out before I could be released!

Into the larger of the two bedrooms we squeezed our double bed. A vast mahogany wardrobe took up most of the space. It seemed as though the room had been built round this piece of furniture, still grand, but now somewhat dilapidated and water-stained as well. It was ideal for holding our clothes, but the remaining floor-space was so limited that only one of us could dress at a time.

The lodge was the gate-house to the School Sanatorium, a stately home a few hundred yards up the drive. Ruling over this domain was a large matron, reputed to be a friendly dragon. Her name was Miss Thomas and she was a saint to us. At any time of the day or night, we could wander up to the warmth of the San., and use the ground-floor bathroom with its two deep, old-fashioned baths conveniently situated side by side. There was a never-ending supply of hot water, and John and I used to lie shoulder-deep in a steamy room. Miss Thomas often invited us to her private suite for a bite of food afterwards, and when the spring came she insisted that we made liberal use of the well-stocked vegetable garden. She also showed me where mushrooms grew in abundance, and told me that local greengrocers would pick them in the early hours of the morning. We lived on free mushrooms and rhubarb. I became an expert at making mushroom and vegetable casserole, mushroom flan, mushroom and cheese with rice – and today we are still mushroom addicts.

Without Matron, I am not sure we could have survived our first two winters at Harrow. She never interfered in our private lives, yet we knew that in a crisis she would be there. Luckily we were never ill, apart from chilblains and the usual winter colds, but had we had anything serious, she would have taken charge at once. She had several trained nurses – who had not heard of union rules. They were always spotlessly dressed in uniform, and their patients were thoroughly spoilt. I heard it said that whenever a patient was admitted, he had to remain in bed for a week for a complete rest. He was not allowed to put a foot on the floor and was given bed-baths twice a day! No wonder it was a popular place. Matron would not tolerate inefficiency, and Harrow must have been one of the few schools which could boast a well-equipped operating-theatre.

When we arrived, in 1955, masters were paid their salary quarterly, the grand total for John at that time being £1 a day with 10% deducted for living accommodation. It seemed grossly unfair that the same amount, 10%, was deducted whether one was living in a condemned house or, more fortunately, in one of Harrow's excellent properties. Later this was altered and accommodation was graded. In order to get a monthly cheque (because we could not last out the quarter), we had to go cap in hand to the Head Master. The first month's salary enabled us to visit Woolworths. We bought a dozen large plastic bowls and yards of waterproof sheeting. These were more or less in constant use in the cottage. Whenever it rained, the water would pour in. Our bedroom was the driest room and only leaked above the wardrobe, so it was quite convenient to leave a bowl permanently on the top. The other containers were dotted over the floors. How quickly one becomes accustomed to furniture placed at odd angles round the room. We were soon so used to stepping over brightly-coloured bowls and hearing the constant splatter of drops into them that we almost took it for granted.

After our first two years at Harrow, a Governor was appointed with special responsibility for the masters. I wrote a letter inviting him to tea. To my delight he accepted and I prayed for rain. I experimented at making meringues and éclairs. When the great day arrived, to my joy the heavens opened, the lightning flashed, the thunder rolled. On the dot of four o'clock a chauffeur-driven car drew up to our cottage, and an immaculate Governor stepped into our sitting-room (there was no hallway). I took his umbrella, put it to drip in one of the bowls, and invited him to sit down.

The Governor played his part well. He sat on one half of the sofa – the other half was covered with waterproof sheeting in the middle of which was a dark pool of rain water. Our plastic bowls were scattered over the floor. My precious cakes sat on a trolley with an antique silver-plated tea service which had been a wedding-present.

Soon all three of us were involved in a serious discussion on the problems of a Communist society. I had to turn off the electric fire as the flex became sodden with rain, and introduce our paraffin stove with exhaust-type fumes belching from it. My cakes were excellent, the silver gleamed, and our baby daughter Siobhan was gurgling in the bedroom.

'Would you like a tour round the cottage?' I asked. I opened one of the four doors leading out of the sitting-room. The Governor squeezed into our bedroom. In the next room he found Siobhan sitting in her cot with her hands stretched out to catch the rain-drops falling from the light bulb. I had not cleaned out the larder for two days, and the mushroom-type fungi which had appeared would have gladdened the eye of any horticulturalist. He washed his hands in the stone sink and glanced at the door-covered bath which was my kitchen table. I thrust his umbrella into his hands saying brightly: 'I am sure that you would like to use the cloak-room.' He duly walked out of the back door into the rain.

The following day the head of the Works department, Mr George Hinton, arrived to ask us to find temporary accommodation for four months, as the workmen were moving in at the end of the week. Well done the Governor!

Four months later we returned to an enlarged cottage – relatively free from damp. My old fungus-ridden larder had been transformed into a new hallway, and we had our own bathroom and indoor loo. The bedrooms had been knocked together and made into a large sitting-room, and two further bedrooms had been built on. All was well until the first storm. John and I lay warmly in our bed, confident that the cottage was dry. Our daughter sang gaily in her bedroom – and continued singing with such gusto that I decided to investigate. I found her sitting in her cot, arms outstretched, staring up at the sky above. There was a full moon, and an abundance of stars and leaves danced in the wind. The roof of her bedroom had blown off. There was rubble all round the cot. Some of the roofing fabric must surely have landed in the cot, but she had casually thrown it out. It seemed a miracle that she was alive, let alone unhurt and in such spirits. During the boring hours of the night (for she hardly ever slept), life had become exciting and new.

When the workmen came a few hours later, they asked: 'She was insured, wasn't she?'

Despite all the upheavals and discomforts of Sanatorium Lodge, we at least had privacy. In later life I have found that privacy is a rare commodity. I yearn to be alone, and today would gladly exchange my luxurious accommodation for the relative discomforts and seclusion of our first home.

When the Senior Chaplain died, we applied for, and were given, his flat, on the first floor of Peterborough Cottage, a beautiful house which stood by a lane leading down to the rugger fields. Our third and final move at Harrow was to the ground-floor flat in the same house. The rooms all had country views. There was a large drawing-room with huge windows leading on to a balcony, and a games room. John had a tiny, but perfect, strangely-shaped study.

Peterborough Cottage was ideal, but during the winter months I found living there a misery. Although it faced south, the lack of central heating meant that I was desperately cold. I shivered so much that my spine gave out, and an orthopaedic surgeon from one of the London teaching hospitals insisted I should wear a steel corset. I also suffer from Raynaud's disease: my nails turn first blue, then whitish grey. I wrote to the Bursar asking for the roof to be lagged, and received an immediate reply: it was not worth lagging the roof as Peterborough Cottage was not centrally heated. To John's astonishment, I replied saying if that was all that was needed before the roof could be lagged, please go ahead and instal central heating. Within days the workmen moved in, a large boiler was installed in the games room – and the roof was lagged. It was not long before the Bursar was inundated with similar requests, and Harrow could boast that all the masters who wished it had central heating.

Peterborough Cottage had a large and beautiful garden with a long, wide lawn surrounded by flower beds, herbaceous borders, peach and apple and pear trees, thick leafy bushes, and our own bluebell wood. Next to it slept the grounds of Peterborough Lodge, where our colleague David Jones lived. His garden was a weird and wonderful wasteland, and had remained untouched this century. Multitudes of rare wild flowers returned annually to greet their respective seasons. Spring produced trumpet-type daffodils, scented narcissi, and sweetly perfumed bell-flowers such as I had never seen. There were lilacs of every shade from white to deep purple, magnolias, rhododendrons, fruit trees ablaze with blossom. Families of birds rebuilt their nests in the same nooks year by year, tranquil and undisturbed. Summer brought the roses. Old, unpruned, wizened rose bushes would unfold their hidden beauty and burst into prolific flower. Large white tea-roses, with a deliciously delicate fragrance, bloomed and re-bloomed all summer long. Then came the mellow shades of autumn leading into the sleep of winter. For squirrels and tortoises the garden was a haven where they could hibernate in peace. The leaves returned into the sequestered earth to fertilise the next generation, leaving the stark trees silhouetted against the sky.

David Jones's room was lit by one of the great windows of Peterborough Lodge. Through this casement he could see an ancient acacia tree, its splendid proportions now immortalised in many of his paintings. How he loved Nature's flowers – and how he hated 'the sods one buys at the florist's' – 'They don't seem to be real flowers any longer.' David's room was organised chaos - his water-colours, prints and calligraphy covered every inch of hanging-space, and the surplus was stacked behind his bed. He seemed to live on China tea, Bath Oliver biscuits, boiled eggs and Marmite. He would sit and reminisce about Welsh or Greek mythology, and then rummage through his collection for a picture he had painted which illustrated the story he was telling. His pictures were all noble and magnificent, but because he would rarely part with any of them, he was better known as an author and poet. David's soul was expressed through his paintings; his poetry was only their translation. He sent me his poem *The Wall*, which won the Harriet Munroe Prize, and asked me to give my comments . . . this I found exceedingly difficult to do. Another poem, *In Parenthesis*, won the Hawthornden Prize. In it he wrote about the horrors of the First World War experienced by people of all walks of life; not only the tragedy and suffering, but also the camaraderie and the love which they found. It was all the more eloquent because he used the raw language of the private soldier.

Not until I heard a radio recording of *In Parenthesis* could I fully appreciate the depth and beauty of David's genius. He moulded the voices together, and the audience shared the affinity, fears, thrills and sorrows which the soldiers experienced in trench warfare. As I read it now, I am part of the turmoil of the First World War.

David himself had served in the trenches. After the battle of the Somme he was collecting firewood for warmth, and glanced through a hole in the wall of a hut to find a Catholic priest celebrating the Eucharist at a makeshift altar. Beyond were some of his hard-drinking, loud-swearing fellow Privates, transformed, so it seemed, and kneeling in the holy Presence of their God. 'I felt immediately the oneness between the Offerant and those toughs that clustered round him in the dim-lit byre. . . .'

David became a Catholic as a result of that encounter. He was devout and holy. I was a particularly welcome visitor when I was pregnant, for he loved to see the contours of a woman with child. He would search through his pictures to show me similar outlines. He considered pregnancy a beautiful state, God's perfect gift to mankind.

When we moved to the first-floor flat at Peterborough Cottage, our neighbours in the ground-floor flat were Ronald Watkins and his wife Bunty. They were quiet people, gentle and cultured, with a dignified charm. Bunty was a professional 'cellist and I loved to hear her practising. On warm sunny days, when the windows were open, the clear sweet sound of the 'cello mingled with the songs of the birds in the garden.

Before he and Bunty moved into Peterborough Cottage, Ronald Watkins had been housemaster of a House known for its family connections. It was both traditional and conservative. On the first day of his housemastership Ronald was greeted by his Head of House, a self-assured young man, who politely conducted him round the building. At the end of the tour the Head of House opened the green baize door which separated the boys' side from the private side, where the housemaster's family had their quarters. 'That is your side,' he said courteously, 'and this is mine. If you want to come through the door, you must let me know first.'

The principle of 'the green baize door' was epitomised by the career of Thomas Henry Steel, housemaster of 'The Grove' from 1855–81. It was said of him that he had never been seen on the boys' side of it. The monitors were expected to maintain control in their own way. In support of this, one housemaster said, 'A boy who can rule a House at nineteen can rule a nation at fifty.' He maintained that the two tasks were equally easy and equally difficult.

But however competent and assured his Head of House may be, a housemaster has to be prepared for almost any eventuality. One of the Harrow housemasters had just completed his first year and was sadly saying farewell to some of his monitors who were leaving to go to university. They were a good group of boys who had led him kindly through the many difficult problems that house-mastering entails. His wife and he were in the drawing-room, ready to offer sherry as the boys came in one by one, clutching photographs of themselves. The giving of these photographs, known as 'leavers', to masters and fellow students who had over the years become one's friends, was a Harrow custom. The housemaster accepted a 'leaver' from an eighteen-year-old Thai, who said:

'I would like to introduce you to my family, who have flown over for a holiday.'

'Of course,' said the housemaster. 'I've not met your family. It will be a pleasure.'

In walked a beautiful pregnant young lady accompanied by a young boy holding the hand of a Thai nanny.

'My wife and son,' said the monitor. Throughout his whole career at Harrow, he had not divulged the fact that he was a father.

Sir Bernard and Lady Docker donated some Daimler cars to Harrow, so that the boys could be taught to drive and could learn the fundamental principles of the motor-car engine. (Presumably they felt that the boys should learn on the type of car they would be likely eventually to own.) The boys were given excellent driving instruction under the guidance of the police.

When the young King Hussein of Jordan went into the senior school, his housemaster asked whether he wanted to put his name down for driving-lessons. He gently declined, saying that he had been driving for some years. 'You see, Sir, a moving target is harder to hit.' There had already been several attempts to assassinate him, in one of which a bullet lodged in a medal which he was wearing. While at Harrow the young king kept an 'illegal' car at a garage in the town. His chauffeur would collect him and drive him away in state; once away from The Hill, the King took over the wheel – all unbeknown to the Harrow staff. His brother, Prince Talal, was also at Harrow. One year he entered for the Imperial History Prize, which John was adjudicating. He wrote a brilliant essay in which he attacked T. E. Lawrence for what he had NOT done for the Arabs, and he won.

A newly-appointed housemaster of a public school was apprehensive at the thought of greeting the boys and parents on the first day of term, and had everything ready long before the first arrivals could be expected. The tension mounted. Eventually someone suggested that he might do some gardening. Donning his wellingtons, he found a spade, rubbed his hands together, and began to dig round the roses under the study window. He turned up the first spadeful of earth, and to his amazement a full bottle of White Horse whisky appeared. He took it into his study, opened it and poured out a tot. It was genuine. He had another one for luck and returned with his spade to the rose bed. Again he drove the spade into the soil; up came another bottle. He found enough drink to keep an alcoholic happy for weeks. There were layers of wine and port neatly buried, lying flat in the earth. Soon his study was full of clay-coated bottles of all shapes and sizes. The study table groaned under their weight. Parents anxious to meet the new housemaster and see what impression he made were greeted by a bewildered and over-happy man who burst into song when they entered.

Late in the evening, when the housemaster was subdued and sleepy, a wealthy young prince returned to his Alma Mater. The sight of the hoard threw him into a state of confusion. Then he smiled. 'I really thought that I had found the ideal hiding-place – I couldn't know you were fond of digging the garden.'

The prince's punishment was to arrange the transport of the bottles to the housemaster's cellar. No doubt he found another hiding-place for any future consignments. The housemaster entertained lavishly for the rest of the year, and the prince remained a monitor.

During our time at Harrow the town was out of bounds, and so were its entertainments, though the films being made and shown in the late fifties and early sixties were far from erotic. The Board of Film Censors applied a far stricter standard then than now and a film would be banned if four-letter words were used or if it included frontal nudity of either sex. By the late seventies erotic films were being freely shown on the open market. The town is no longer out of bounds, and monitors may be sent to 'stand guard' outside the cinemas. The other night I had dinner with a man who told me that his son had recently accepted a challenge from another boy in his House. He was to visit a cinema in the town which was showing a particularly erotic and pornographic film. The boy put on his dark glasses, smoothed down his hair with oil, donned a polo-necked shirt, and successfully paid for his ticket. He sat near the back of the stalls. He had never seen such 'goings on'. If this was adult life, what was the point of education, of discipline and training? His eyes goggled at first, but presently he became bored. Still, he sat on, and with the help of the odd Russian cigarette time passed. The lights came up at the end of the show: to his utter amazement, he found that he had been sitting beside a middle-aged master from the school. Old and young looked at each other, nodded slowly, and walked out of different exits. Nothing more was ever said.

Among the students at Harrow in our time was a young man of eighteen. His parents were very precise; nothing in their house was out of place – each magazine had its own place on the 'casual' table. On one occasion they had introduced us to some of their friends, and thought we were out of earshot: I heard them say, 'John and Daphne Rae – it really is rather disgusting, she is pregnant again – they breed like rabbits.' Their son had just completed his last 'A'-level exam. He wanted to go to Oxford, but his father, who insisted on being called by his Territorial Army rank, wanted him to go to Sandhurst. The son wanted to read English, play in the orchestra, and act; his father wanted him to read anything *but* English and play games, nothing too soft – preferably rugger. 'A' levels over, the boy learned that Yehudi Menuhin was going to play in the Royal Festival Hall in London. To escape from the confines of Harrow on a warm summer evening was tempting: to listen to the Brahms Violin Concerto was irresistible. He dared not ask for permission as he had already been 'gated' for another offence. He took the risk and on his return was caught by his housemaster. The next day he was expelled: his parents were shattered. This eighteen-year-old young man was locked in his bedroom, and remained there till the end of term. His parents never spoke to him throughout this time. At mealtimes the door was unlocked and his food was handed in to him. It was a prison game: the rules had to be observed. In the end, in spite of his parents' attitude, the young man went to Oxford and succeeded in his Arts degree. His was one of the few cases of expulsion during our time at Harrow.

However rare expulsion may be at a school, there is frequently an upward surge during the first few weeks of a new headmastership. Consciously or unconsciously, the retiring headmaster may allow discipline to deteriorate. His successor must act immediately if he is to take control of his school. When Dr Norwood took over at Harrow in 1926, he expelled forty boys in the first week. John has also had to expel during the first term of each of his two headmasterships. In one of the schools it was on account of drug abuse. I wholeheartedly agree with his principle of immediate expulsion for any boy who is caught 'pushing' any type of drug, whether it is hard or soft. We did not suffer from the problem of drug abuse during our eleven years at Harrow – indeed, I do not think the boys would have seen anything sinister in the story of my trip with the opium-users on the rafts in Siam. Pot-smoking did not become a popular pastime in schools until the middle sixties. Only during recent years have Eastern countries realised that there is a ready market in Britain for the sale of marijuana and heroin; and only very recently have young people in general had the money to buy these drugs.

The secret of keeping boarding-school boys out of trouble is to keep them fully occupied. Harrow had superb sports facilities and its own excellent farm. There were also the school plays.

Ronald Watkins is known in Shakespearian circles the world over for his lectures and readings. A great producer, he would stage a Shakespeare play each year at Harrow. These were great events, and were worth the long hours of rehearsal. Boys, masters and parents take a pride in the school when a play is well performed – and all Ronald Watkins's productions were excellent. More important, perhaps, is the fact that a play of such calibre involves so many boys, both on the stage and behind the scenes. Electricians and artists can show their skills, as can assistant producers and directors. A unique comradeship brings together boys of different age groups and interests, away from the House system. Hidden talents come to light. I have always maintained that a small minority of boys can release pent-up emotions on the stage, acting their parts to the full as they act out their dream world – and they need an audience for this to be effective. If this outlet were denied them, they could become aggressive or over-emotional, or perhaps lonely and friendless.

111

Harrow is only ten miles from the cultural centre of London, and sometimes a master would gather a group of boys, book seats for a theatre or concert, and enjoy a good evening. Unfortunately not many masters were willing to do this. We heard tales of well-intentioned staff taking twenty or so boys to the theatre, to find when the lights came up at the interval that there were only a few left. A master who 'policed' the boys by sitting behind them might dictate that no, absolutely no, liquor could be consumed at the interval – and yet he would be confronted by a young man staggering to his seat having knocked back several tots, to spend the rest of the play hiccoughing or asleep. Perhaps John and I were fortunate, or made a wise choice of good plays or films, but as far as I remember only one boy disappeared during a performance and returned to the Underground the worse for wear. Our rule was: 'Yes, go to the bar at the interval, and have a drink – but only one – and you are to be in your seat after the first bell.'

In my own schooldays in Perthshire our headmistress allowed us to visit any cinema or theatre on a Saturday. The only condition was that we had to write down where we intended to go. As she trusted us, we never let her down, and to this day I value the free-dom we had. In my last year at school, this good lady was succeeded by a new, efficient and intolerable woman, who not only refused to allow us past the front gates, but made a rule that we were not to speak to the two Polish gardeners – both well into their seventies. Our freedom had been suddenly curtailed, and we reacted by playing truant.

I believe that trust is essential. Young men and women working for university places are under great strain and pressure. Their intellectual life is at its peak and they must surely be treated as mature and reliable people.

Apart from the excursions to London, there were regular film shows at Harrow in Speech Room. Whether the master choosing the films had excellent taste, or whether the boys welcomed any-thing that might relieve boredom, the shows were popular. John is an avid film addict, and would always be one of the first to arrive for any performance. (He tells me that a film depicting life at the school was once shown to the boys; they collapsed with un-controlled laughter, much to the chagrin of the producer and director.) The film shows started with the inevitable cartoon, and John would sit with tears pouring down his face in helpless laugh-ter. My sense of humour – and I do have one – lies dormant during

Mickey Mouse and McGoo, so I would creep in later, fumbling my way to my seat in time for the main feature.

In the early years of our marriage, just after the first prizes were awarded in the Premium Bond draw, my mother-in-law won what was then the top prize – £1,000. She had jokingly said that if ever she won this prize, she would give each child £100. John knew exactly what he would spend this windfall on. We were one of the first families in the school to possess a television – John's idea of luxury. Some of our acquaintances thought it was beneath them to own such a time-waster; to my amusement, as years went by they bought a set 'for the children' or 'for our elderly parents'. Yet I am distressed to realise how much of a time-waster it truly is. I rarely watch it – and hence I miss many an excellent programme.

Because the boys spent their afternoons enjoying the sports facilities or working on the farm, there was a class before breakfast each day, and 'Late School' on three evenings a week, to make up the number of lessons. 'Late School' finished at 7.30 p.m. The most difficult period to teach was on Friday evening at the end of a long week.

One term, during our later period at Harrow when John had successfully transferred from Maths to History, he was rather surprised to find his History class assembled and ready in good time for this end-of-the-week period. John taught with his back turned to a large window which overlooked a passageway between two tall drab buildings. The boys always seemed attentive and in a particularly happy frame of mind. This degree of interest continued until one evening a boy in the class made a sound of deep satisfaction. John noticed that all the alert faces had developed smiles, and seemed to be gazing through the window. He turned and saw the view that had held the attention of these seventeen-year-olds for so long. At the window of the house across the passageway were three girls with little or nothing on, making seductive gestures. The house was privately owned, and had recently become a weekend brothel. It was not John's fine, stimulating teaching which had been holding the attention of the form. The brothel was closed immediately. I doubt whether any boys had taken advantage of it – brothels exist for middle-aged men.

I was frequently pregnant during the first decade of my married life. In my schooldays, I would have been embarrassed to be seen talking to a pregnant woman, but I never experienced any awkwardness with the students at Harrow. Living on The Hill, I had often to carry heavy shopping up from the town, and if I met one of the boys he would offer to carry the bags. Perhaps there was an ulterior motive for in those days I enjoyed cooking and took pride in what I produced. There were always home-made cakes, biscuits and coffee to refresh us.

Because John absolutely refused to use a lawn-mower or any garden tool, I made an enormous sherry chocolate cake every week and on Sundays there was a free tea for any boy willing to come and help keep the weeds at bay. It was a happy time, and the results were beautiful. Our friendly dustman, the father of thirteen, used to bring his shears to cut our huge rambling hedge – in order, so he said, to facilitate removing the dustbin for emptying. Every year I gave him one of John's old suits as a thank-you. He would change into the new clothing immediately and show off to John when he appeared at the end of a lesson. 'Thank you, Sir, your wife has just given me this. Fine fit, isn't it, Sir?' and he would parade in the centre of the road, proud as a peacock, with the traffic and the boys milling round him.

I never locked the front door of Peterborough Cottage, the reason being that until this day John is incapable of keeping a key safe in his pocket, and security isn't worth seeing him 'lose his cool' while perching precariously at the end of a ladder, trying to squeeze through a window. Coming home on Sunday afternoons, heavily pregnant, tired from Harrow's steep hill, longing for privacy and to throw my body on to a sofa in order to recover my breath, I would find our drawing-room chairs occupied, the *Times* crossword partially finished, and the boys greeting me: 'We've laid the table for tea, Mrs Rae, and brought in the high chair. Shall we put the kettle on now?' My distress quickly gave way to appreciation, and John and I would sit down in the drawing-room surrounded by a happy group.

During the Summer Term before the final 'A'-level exams, John held 'open house' for his students at six in the morning. If the weather was fine, they took deck chairs into the garden, and revision lessons were held there to the amazement of the milkman, the paperboy, and no doubt the cows in the field next to our garden. The boys were incredibly grateful, and the numbers grew, as friends of pupils took advantage of this extra, free tuition. The subject in which the need for revision was greatest was usually English Literature. At that time it was a 'Cinderella' subject. Not a single master at Harrow had read English at university. John became very unpopular among the rest of the staff when in desperation he put up a notice on the Masters' Common Room board, to say in effect that English was a serious subject and not to be treated in an offhand manner. Furious masters complained to the Head about this 'audacious fellow'. The same evening John received a telephone call, he was to go immediately to the Head Master's study.

'I should be angry,' Dr James said, 'but you are quite right, we need good English teaching here.' Jeremy Lemmon, an Old Harrovian fresh from university, with a good English Literature degree, was appointed to the staff.

In *My Early Life*, Winston Churchill recalled being taught at Harrow by Robert Somervell, a teacher of genius:

'By being so long in the lowest form I gained an immense advantage over the cleverer boys. They all went on to learn Latin and Greek and splendid things like that. But I was taught English. We were considered such dunces that we could only learn English. Mr Somervell – a most delightful man, to whom my debt is great – was charged with the duty of teaching the stupidest boys the most disregarded thing – namely, to write mere English. He knew how to do it. He taught it as no one else has ever taught it. Not only did we learn English parsing thoroughly, but we also practised continually English analysis. Mr Somervell had a system of his own. He took a fairly long sentence and broke it up into its components by means of black, red, blue and green inks. Subject, verb, object: Relative Clauses, Conditional Clauses, Conjunctive and Disjunctive Clauses! Each had its colour and its bracket. It was a kind of drill. We did it almost daily. As I remained in the Third Fourth three times as long as anyone else, I had three times as much of it. I learned it thoroughly. Thus I got into my bones the essential structure of the ordinary British sentence – which is a noble thing. And when in after years my schoolfellows who had won prizes and distinction for writing such beautiful Latin poetry and pithy Greek epigrams had to come down again to common English, to earn their living or make their way, I did not feel myself at any disadvantage. Naturally I am biassed in favour of boys learning English. I would make them all learn English: and then I would let the clever ones learn Latin as an honour, and Greek as a treat. But the only thing I would whip them for is not knowing English. I would whip them hard for that. . . .'[10]

Family

When one looks back on the past, it is the summer days one immediately remembers. I find myself recalling summer holidays at Harrow when we had picnic breakfasts on our south-facing wooden balcony, overlooking our garden and the copse which separated us from the school farm. There the cows, moon-faced and bleary-eyed from their night's rest, watched us whilst they lazily chewed the cud. Beyond lay London – but we were too far away to hear the hum of traffic on the busy main roads. We would pack a picnic lunch and walk across the fields clutching baskets of fresh food, fruit and home-made lemonade. We were addicts of Ducker – and where else in Britain would we have had such a magnificent swimming-pool to ourselves on a hot summer's day? Some of the married masters at Harrow were wise and provident enough to invest in a small country property which could be used as a future refuge in retirement and a present escape in the holidays; we found it difficult enough to meet the gas and electricity bills without contemplating mortgage repayments as well. But we were young, and the children were healthy, and retirement loomed in the far distance.

Before our marriage we had planned on having six children, and I was depressed to find after three months of marriage that I had not conceived. We made our way to a fertility consultant.

'How long have you been trying to have a child?' she asked.

'Three months,' was my solemn reply.

She repressed her laughter, and later it was found that my

Fallopian tubes were blocked. Once they had been cleared, I became pregnant immediately.

'Typical of you,' said the consultant when she gave me the good news, 'your baby is due on April the first.'

Siobhan made us April fools and eighteen days later she had still not arrived. Good Friday fell on April 19 that year, 1957, and I managed my first nine holes on Walton Heath golf course. I must have been at a low ebb, for I loathe playing golf. When I was at school a professional offered to take three 'outstanding' pupils, and the best all-round games players were presented to him, given a golf club and told to 'swing it'. I swung with gay abandon, and he immediately picked me as his first and only choice. During the next several weeks I chased a ball miserably round Perth golf course, surely one of the coldest in the country. I hit hard and fast, hoping with luck to be back in school in time for tea. I was too successful – the professional was delighted with my progress; but I could not find any enthusiasm for the game, much preferring gymnastics, hockey and tennis. I failed to persuade our Games mistress that I was an utter loss at golf, and that my slap-happy attitude would never turn me into an international player. One night I lay in bed listening to a gale and thinking, 'Surely a game is not a game if one loathes playing it.' With this great philosophical revelation I sprang out of bed, made my way to the Head Mistress's study, and found her reading the *Scotsman* with a glass of wine on the table beside her. It was 1.00 a.m. 'Hallo Daphne, what can I do for you?' she said casually as I opened the door. I explained my dilemma, shared the remainder of the bottle of wine, and returned to bed confident that I would never have to face a golf course again. But here I was, nearly nine and three-quarter months pregnant, winning my first match since my early teens. It obviously shook my system, and resulted in my daughter's birth at dawn on Easter Saturday.

I had absolutely no idea how to cope with a babe. I was convinced that it would all come naturally. I would not be pushed into reading books about what might go wrong, firmly believing that nothing *would* go wrong, and refused to worry about weighing-scales. My dear friend Elizabeth, a midwife and nurse, who had trained in a very modern clinic in Switzerland, came to stay and made dozens of specially-shaped nappies tied with tapes (which lasted all my six children); she thought that safety-pins, essential for conventional nappies, should be made illegal.

Siobhan was an easy but exhausting child. We used to creep into her room during her first days and weeks of life, holding a candle in order to see if she was asleep, but we would always find her with her eyes wide open. She was nearly six months old when we first saw her asleep, and then I was so frightened that I shook her, fearing that she had died. She has made up for this in later life, and now I have to strip the clothes off her bed and threaten her with a cold sponge in order to get her up in time for work.

I taught Siobhan to read early. An aunt gave her three Beatrix Potter books on her third birthday and was amazed to find that she had read them all – without fault – by breakfast. One was *Peter Rabbit* which she thoroughly enjoyed. She had just one question: 'What does "soporific" mean, Mother?' I also taught her some Maths; she knew her tables and had started enjoying Algebra, when she was admitted to her first school, a week after her third birthday. My doctor was convinced that Siobhan was exhausting me, particularly as I was breast-feeding another baby, and insisted that we should try sending her to school. The other pupils ranged from four years old up to eight. So, at the beginning of the summer term, I delivered an excited Siobhan to school for her first half-day. At midday, I went to collect my beloved daughter, having been desperately worried about her all the morning, and found myself surrounded by other young mothers collecting their four-year-olds. All the children – bar mine – came running out into the garden, and I was left alone searching the passages. Eventually the Head Mistress saw me and apologised. 'I'm so sorry, Mrs Rae, I completely forgot about Siobhan – please follow me.' Siobhan had started the morning with the four-year-olds, but had moved rapidly up from class to class. She remained at this school until she was eight years old, and to this day she says that she has done very little work since.

Penelope, my second child, was due in early December, 1959. On December 17, the last evening of term, I was nearly two weeks overdue, but end-of-term House dinners, particularly Christmas ones, were not to be missed. Great preparations were made, with holly on the walls, the Christmas tree alight with candles, crackers on the tables, and a feast of a meal. Turkey would be served, with all the trimmings, and Chef would bring in a pudding, ablaze with brandy and topped with holly, its leaves and berries curling together in the sizzling heat. There would be wine and port for the senior boys and plenty of cider for the younger ones. That year we had been invited to dinner by John Morgan, housemaster at 'Moreton's', and his wife Joan. Feeling very fit and looking forward to a happy dinner party with the boys, I spent a hectic morning at Marks & Spencers, battling my way through the Christmas crowds and carrying, or rather holding, Siobhan as she sat on top of my highly pregnant stomach. Later I had to telephone Joan Morgan and say that as I had started labour, I didn't think I could come to dinner, but John would be there, so please send my portion of turkey and mince pies back with him. When he returned without them, I was furious.

Penelope was a hand presentation – one that is thought to make natural delivery impossible. My midwife and doctor pleaded with me to go into hospital, but my labour was already far advanced and I argued that the baby might not survive the journey. They agreed reluctantly, and shortly afterwards Penelope arrived easily and well, with me squatting on the floor 'Thai' fashion. She was a beautiful babe and has grown into a beautiful adult.

I owed my good fortune in being able to follow the Thai method for Penelope's birth to the period when I was living in Thailand with my mother and stepfather. On my first night in Bangkok I noticed something moving behind the large wardrobe. I thought it was a snake, so I quietly crawled out of bed and went downstairs to find one of the house servants. Arming himself with a piece of bamboo, he returned with me and eased the wardrobe away from the wall. When he saw the large lizard-like reptile he immediately fell to his knees and touched the floor with his head. I understood that it was a rare creature, and considered holy. Although large, it was harmless, and remained happily in my room until I left the country.

One result of this was that my presence was felt to be a good omen, and I was asked to be present whenever a birth was imminent in the compound. It was to be one of my greatest joys, and I became very knowledgeable over the natural way of giving birth. A Thai woman in labour was surrounded by her family. When she had a contraction she would stay still, concentrating on her muscles and her breathing. When the child's head was about to be crowned, she squatted on the floor, and holding the head gently in her hands, guided the body around. It was all so easy, and there was not a sign of fear. The women were all relaxed and happy, and as they did not push in the last stages of labour, they were not exhausted. I am sure that the ease of giving birth was due to the squatting position. This is the position Eastern people adopt when sitting, and so their muscles are naturally relaxed and supple. I never saw a difficult birth, and I never heard anyone cry out in pain. It still frightens me to think that Penelope might have died if that strange reptile had not taken up residence in my bedroom.

The consequences of sharing my room with this reptile were without exception beneficial. I was treated as a goddess, always the first to be served at table and given the pick of the food. Creased sheets were replaced by clean ones, even if I had lain down on my bed for no more than five minutes. Each time I had my bath, my faithful servant would hold up a spotless towel ready to wrap round me. New underwear, immaculately folded, would be placed on the chair. As a sign of respect, he insisted on being always at a lower level than myself and would, if necessary, shuffle on his knees to achieve this, no matter how many other people were present. Fortunately he was very small, so this only became necessary if I sat on a low chair.

My time in the Far East seems like another existence now, but to it we owe Penelope's life. She was the first of our children to be christened at Harrow, in the crypt of the School Chapel. Her god-father was Peter Searle, who had been best man at our wedding. He brought a shell which he filled with water – both from the Holy Land. It was a beautiful service. John's very elderly and deaf grandparents were in the family party, and after the ceremony we had tea in the Masters' Common Room. Great-Grandmother called me over to her:

'Daphne, the waiter is not doing his job – he is standing talking to the other guests. You really must have a word with him.'

The waiter, dressed in tails, was one of our guests, the head boy, John Harvey. (The Harvey family needs no introduction to wine-lovers.) I had my word with John, and he played his role with dignity.

Our third daughter, Alyce, arrived on June 18, 1961; by this time we had moved into Peterborough Cottage. She was born on a Sunday, at lunchtime, between pudding and coffee, and on the following day I attended an anniversary lunch at Moreton's House. I sat opposite a gentle couple in a marquee in the garden. When we were introduced, the man said to my husband:

'My son Hugh has just told me that your wife had a baby on Sunday. I thought he meant yesterday, but it must have been a week ago.'

'No, it was yesterday – about twenty-two hours ago.'

'Good heavens,' he said, turning to me, 'I am a gynaecologist in Cardiff. I want you to come down and meet all my pregnant mothers – it would be good for them.'

Alyce was born with long dark hair, which was plaited after her first bath. I toyed with the idea of calling her Ursula as she had a down of thickish hair over her entire body. When she was eleven months old, my father-in-law, a radiologist, and a friend of his, a general surgeon, met in our flat over lunch. They watched Alyce move across the sitting-room in her own unique way. Both men looked at each other, went into a huddle, and then said that Alyce must be X-rayed immediately, as they were convinced that she had a dislocated hip. 'No one could possibly use their limbs the way she does,' I was told, 'and have normal joints.' Plans were made to book her into the Westminster Children's Hospital (where John's father had once worked), and a paediatric surgeon was telephoned. The following day we were informed that the X-rays were normal.

When Alyce was about three years old, a master found her eating a very strange-looking toadstool. He took it away from her and gave me the remnants. I took her to Harrow Hospital, where she was made to vomit. With sirens wailing and lights flashing, an ambulance rushed the remnants of the toadstool to Guy's Hospital where they could be identified – Guy's being the only hospital in London with a Poisons Department. We were soon told that the toadstool was an extremely rare variety, and deadly poisonous. By this time, Alyce was lying unconscious. At Guy's recommendation, she was transferred from Harrow to Edgware Hospital where a respirator was available. When we arrived a Hungarian doctor took John aside, and when John asked what would happen if the toadstool was indeed poisonous, he said haltingly: 'The heart – it stops.'

Guy's Hospital had meanwhile arranged for a special serum to be sent by air from Geneva. A police car brought it from the airport. I was amazed and delighted that Guy's emergency plans were put into action so quickly and so effectively.

A week after the incident, the remains of the toadstool were taken to the Royal Botanical Gardens for a second opinion, and we were told that she could have eaten a plateful of them without ill-effect. Today, Alyce is alive and well – her collapse at the hospital was due to the effects of the violent measures necessary to make her sick, and the prolonged vomiting itself.

Emily's birth occurred five weeks later than expected. She was so long overdue that I had a disturbing letter from the authorities asking my doctor to confirm that I was pregnant, as I had well exceeded my free ante-natal milk allowance. She was born on April 30, 1963, weighing nearly eleven pounds, and having arrived, refused to go to sleep unless she was being held in my arms.

She is remembered by the Fire Brigade for two emergencies. One day she was riding her tricycle which had lost the rubber grip on the handle bar. She decided to push her finger into the hole at the end of the bar – and there it stayed. Still attached to the tricycle, she was sitting at the dining-table casually eating her lunch when the firemen arrived. Emily and her tricycle were soon parted.

The second occasion was more dramatic. We were half-way across a busy High Street when Emily saw a manhole cover with a hole in it. She bent down and stuck her finger in the hole – and there, once again, it stayed. Police arrived, a crowd gathered, suggestions were made, a woman brought a bottle of olive oil and poured it over her finger joints, and sweets and ice-cream were brought to entice her away. But she was stuck. The summer traffic had to be diverted, I was convulsed with laughter, the *au pair* was distraught. Emily sat unconcerned, eating the sweets and ice-cream with her right forefinger firmly planted in the road. Eventually the Fire Brigade arrived and produced a drill, the piece of road was removed – and Emily considered herself a heroine.

On the first Sports Day at her kindergarten school, John and I watched with pride as our youngest daughter won all the races with considerable ease. We felt very swollen-headed as we accepted the congratulations of other parents. Eventually the last race was to be run, and there stood Emily at the starting-line, her chest covered with the red ribbons she had been awarded for her previous races. A small boy came over to her, and whispered something in her ear. A look of startled concern appeared on her face, and she immediately walked away from the starting-line. A whistle was blown, and a mistress brought her back, protesting. The little boy again came over to her and whispered. Emily stood to attention, and stared straight in front of her.

'Take your marks . . . get ready . . .' and off went the starting-gun.

Emily remained standing to attention – there was not a flicker of movement in her eyes as all the other children dashed across the field. It was as though she had been hypnotised. A teacher spoke to her but received no response. I ran across to her.

'Emily, whatever is the matter with you – why aren't you running?' The race had just finished.

'Mother,' she replied, relaxing for the first time, 'that boy said he wanted to win this race, and that if I moved from this line, he would deaden me, and I didn't want to be deaded yet.'

When I became pregnant yet again, I found that people had gone beyond the stage of congratulations, and had started to commiserate instead. But I was happy to be pregnant, and when I had a sudden miscarriage in my third month I was naturally upset. The doctor examined me, and said that there was another babe still there.

'I will arrange for this to be removed,' she said.

Two gynaecologists confirmed her decision. I spent the next few days trying to convince them all that I was going to have this babe. I knew that I was healthy enough to cope, and if the child was physically or mentally affected – as was the medical opinion – I would face this when it was born. Emily had been a big baby, and the doctors agreed that this, too, was a dangerous omen. But no matter what the difficulties, I could not agree to murder – and murder it would be. The life inside me was lent to me by God, and nothing in this world could make me exterminate it.

I had to find a Roman Catholic gynaecologist who would accept me as his patient – Mr Vincent O'Sullivan. He insisted that I went into St Teresa's Nursing Home, at Wimbledon, where I had the most luxurious room available. Mr O'Sullivan knew that I had little money. The nuns – and he – refused any payment. 'It has been such fun having you,' they said, and certainly I thoroughly enjoyed being there. There was no proselytising, just the nuns living with God and expressing love through their example. If the problems of this pregnancy had not come, I might never have experienced the joy and peace which I have known over these last years since I became a Roman Catholic. My first steps in this direction were taken after being part of this community.

On July 10, 1966, my unidentical twin sons were born with great ease, one weighing 7 pounds 4 ounces, the other 7 pounds 14 ounces. They were in excellent health and well formed. The younger was placed in an incubator, as he had been a breech birth, but he was taken out after only a few minutes as he was so lively that the nurses thought he would break the glass. Had I not miscarried in the third month I would have given birth to triplets. We named our elder son Shamus (Siobhan persuaded me to use this spelling instead of 'Seamus' – she said that her great problem at school was the pronunciation of her name); and the younger, born seven minutes after him, we named Jonathan.

The twins were born at the end of a very busy summer term. John had accepted a new post and was trying to get used to the idea of leaving Harrow. He was also convinced that he was seriously ill. He finds it very difficult to visit anyone in a hospital or nursing-home, and when I started in labour with the twins, I had to drive myself from Harrow to Wimbledon as John was either too nervous or too tired – or perhaps both. But he was with me for the birth, and stayed for a few minutes before going on to a dinner party which was being given by his parents to welcome his brother back from America. Afterwards he went away for a fortnight's rest. His medical brother, Angus, took pity on me, and visited me every day while I was in the nursing-home. After a few days, one of the nuns said that she had something very embarrassing to ask me.

'One Dr Rae came with you when you first arrived, and we haven't seen him since, and another Dr Rae has been visiting you each day – we are all anxious to know which one is your husband?'

When Emily was born the Home Help supervisor from the local council came to interview John.

'Do you know how to use your washing-machine?' she asked him.

'I don't think we own a washing-machine,' he replied. (We had had a washing-machine for some years, but John had ignored its existence through lack of interest.)

'Do you cook with electricity or gas?' the supervisor persisted.

'I have no idea.'

She went into the kitchen to find out for herself.

'I will send you my best help,' the sympathetic lady told me, and Mrs Taft arrived. She was wonderful. A Yorkshire woman who has as sane a mind as anyone I know, 'Taffy' immediately became part of the family. She eventually gave up her council job and came to me for a 'peppercorn' salary.

Taffy's widowed mother was her idol. Her father had been

burnt to death while repairing a boiler, and – almost unbelievably – his body was returned to his wife in a wheelbarrow, in the early hours of the morning, wrapped in sackcloth. His wife coped with little or no money, rising before dawn to dressmake and retiring late to bed after a day of boiling the clothes, starching, baking bread, gardening, scrubbing and cleaning the cottage, and working for her neighbours who were worse off than herself – for she had her health, and guts. Because she could not afford a doctor, she once sewed back her severed finger and made her own splint, after an accident. 'Just with an ordinary needle and thread,' said Taffy.

Taffy's own motto was 'It's a great life if you don't weaken.' 'You can't do to others what you won't do to yourself,' she said. Nothing ever got her down – apart from cricket. Her husband Cliff was a good cricketer, and played for his firm's First XI. At the start of one summer season, he arrived for the opening match. When he unpacked his bag he found that Taffy had cut his new white flannels up to the knee. On a second occasion she unravelled the sleeves of his cricket jumper. After that he kept his cricketing clothes at the office to ensure their safety. Only Taffy could do such outrageous things and make her husband see the funny side of them – which he did. We all dearly loved this tiny dark-haired woman. Whenever we felt low she could lift our spirits. She it was who persuaded the Electricity Board and the Telephone Company not to disconnect us when the bills were unpaid, and on another occasion I found her guarding the gas meter as an irate man from the Gas Board wanted to cut the gas off at the mains. We eventually persuaded him to have a glass of sherry and one of Taffy's cakes. She had talked John into being responsible for the accounts, but John's invariable method of dealing with bills, especially the sort that arrive undisguised in brown envelopes, is to put them unopened in the wastepaper basket. 'Nay, I know when I'm beaten, Mrs Rae,' Taffy told me, and once again, unwillingly, I was in charge of the cheque book.

Taffy had the rare gift of fortitude – she taught us much and although she would find it hard to believe, she has influenced our lives. When we find problems irritating – whether major or minor – we ask 'What would Taffy have done?' At the last service of term this year (Summer, 1982) John's homily in Westminster Abbey was on Taffy.

Taffy came into our lives at a hectic time. Even before my twins were born I had four children to look after, and besides the duties of being a master's wife I was working at a local home for unmarried mothers. My first task there had been to sort out the mice droppings from a half-empty sack of rice. The kitchens were filthy, and I gathered a few highly pregnant girls to help me clean the place up. Here I had my first introduction to adult lesbianism – not in the rather beautiful and idealistic form which can exist in schools and elsewhere, but a far more demanding physical affair. The formidable matron would take an unfortunate mother into her bedroom, make her undress, and then would examine her breasts for an unnecessary length of time. On some evenings, she would make a girl get into bed with her. The girls she picked on were particularly vulnerable and had nowhere else to go. There was little I could do, except perhaps approach the governors. They gathered once a week at the Home, to go to Holy Communion. The girls and I would be ordered to cut wafer-thin bread for dainty sandwiches to be served with coffee. Matron stood over us, supervising our every movement. I plucked up the courage to approach one of the august members. She looked the youngest, and was the only one who walked without a stick, but it proved to be an unfortunate choice – she was deaf. 'Speak up dear, I find it difficult to understand you – what are you talking about – are you trying to tell me that you are unhappy here . . .?' So that was no use. My Swiss friend Elizabeth tried to contact the Chairman, but no one wanted to know.

The girls were a brave lot – from all walks of life – and should not have had to cope with extra sexual problems at this stage. They had their problems with the matron, and the short cut to the house was through St Mary's Churchyard which, in those days, was the popular place for men to expose themselves.

It was a depressing Home in many ways. One of my jobs was to teach the girls psychoprophylaxis – breathing and relaxation – and they asked whether they could come to the cottage for their classes. Boys arriving in search of John had to step over highly pregnant tummies as they made their way across the room. They never batted an eyelid.

I taught the girls my own method of natural childbirth – after Pierre Vallet. Obviously it worked well, for one girl proudly announced that she had had her baby in record time. 'I still had my snow boots on when the baby was born.' The staff at the maternity hospital soon adopted the habit of asking girls in labour if they had been trained by me: if the answer was 'yes', they were taken immediately to the delivery room.

A number of the unmarried mothers wanted to have their babies adopted. Unfortunately one of the almoners at the hospital had herself been adopted as a child, and had been most unhappy. She would ignore, or be downright rude to, any unmarried mother who wanted her babe adopted. I remember a spinster mother aged forty, who greatly loved the father of her child. She wished the little one to be taken away at birth and given to a family who would care for and love him. This request was refused, and she had to spend a heart-breaking six weeks with her son. She asked me to care for the child as she loved him so much. I would go in early each morning to feed and bath the baby. The mother felt in her heart that by offering him for adoption she was giving him the right future, and she did not change her mind. The painful six weeks ended at last, and I was with her when we took him for adoption.

So ho! So ho!
May the courtiers sing,
Honour and life
To Willow the King.

Playing-Fields

Willow the King is a monarch grand,
Three in a row his courtiers stand.
Every day when the sun shines bright
The doors of his palace are painted white,
And all the company bow their backs
To the King with his collar of cobbler's wax.

Willow, King Willow, thy guard hold tight,
Trouble is coming before the night!
Hopping and galloping, short and strong,
Comes the Leathery Duke along;
And down the palaces tumble fast
When once the Leathery Duke gets past.

Throughout the years when I lustily sang this Harrow song, I had no idea what the words stood for: they have recently been translated for me by my husband. I now know that bats are made of willow, and the Leathery Duke is the cricket ball; then the other words fall into place.

'Willow the King' was written by Edward Bowen, assistant master at Harrow for forty-two years until his retirement in 1901. He was an enthusiastic supporter of the Philathletic Club, founded in 1853 by the senior boys at Harrow to encourage athleticism. Bowen was an untiring athlete and apparently thought little of walking from Cambridge to London. As well as being a great performer himself – he played football at the age of sixty-five, within weeks of his death – he was also a great inspiration to others. His strength was in organising team games – he was unenthusiastic over individualistic sporting activities such as racquets and fives. 'I offer it as my deliberate opinion,' he said, 'that the best boys are on the whole the players of games.' Living conditions in his House were spartan, with little comfort such as armchairs and fires. The only luxury allowed – and this was just to encourage the boys – was 'glorification' or 'consolation' cake for House game teas. In the archives of Harrow is a photograph which shows a tea party in progress on the lawns of his House in 1895 – the boys are immaculately dressed and the table laden with food.

I am not a cricket fan – I am far too impatient – but I was persuaded to bowl in the one and only cricket match my school played. It was against a local well-known independent school for boys. I cannot remember how I bowled or how many runs I made, but I do remember that we won the match. Their Games master was furious, the boys' dignity was shaken, and we were not asked for a fixture again.

How seriously should cricket be taken? I fully understand the camaraderie which team games engender, but on the rare occasions when I have watched cricket it has seemed a lonely game, team spirit only really appearing among the side waiting to bat as players lounge and chat in the pavilion. I once spent a delightful day at Winchester watching part of a two-day cricket match against Harrow. It was certainly relaxing – the sun shone, the views were perfect, the deck chairs comfortable and the company excellent, and there were meringues and éclairs in the pavilion during the break for tea. Perhaps this is a good training for the day when we retire at an early age, to make way for the younger generation. However, is this what hard-pressed parents pay for – that their son, or even daughter, should spend so many hours during the week, and such a proportion of the weekend, on the cricket pitch? The Public Schools Commission was informed by one school captain that the average cricketer spent fifteen hours a week playing, while the more enthusiastic, 'who certainly did next to no school work', devoted twenty hours to cricket each week. I entirely agree that there is a time for work and a time for play, but when Oxford and Cambridge are demanding three Grade-A results in 'A' levels for entrance into university to read the more popular subjects, surely more time should be given to work – though not necessarily or exclusively to the examination subjects. I am convinced that unless a student has a brilliant mind, academic work becomes far too narrow. I had lunch recently with the

Admissions Tutor of an Oxford college on the first day of the Christmas Term. He surprised me when he said:

'I have just spent the morning with the freshmen. It has been exhausting and disappointing – they are uneducated and dull.'

My reaction was to ask what grades they had to obtain for entrance into this select college.

'Oh, the majority have three Grade-A's – but they can't conduct a conversation on anything other than their own subject – they're so dull and narrow, it is depressing.'

I feel that the extra time devoted to cricket – a lengthy period because a match lasts so long – could be usefully spent in broadening one's mind. Gone are the days recalled by Arnold Lunn in *Come What May, c.* 1907, when 'the Homeric heroes disported themselves at ease during the hours set aside for homework, while the local intelligentsia did their homework for them'. Such was a hero called Cadby, who used on Saturday evenings to raffle his preparation for the week. In fairness to Edward Bowen, I should add that he fully realised the need for study; his song 'Jack and Joe' (1876) urges Scholar Jack and Sportsman Joe 'Let neither grammar nor bats be lack; let brains with sinews grow.' Nevertheless the school attitude to cricket was summarised in 1866 by the magazine *Tyro*: 'If there is one thing that *lives* more than another at Harrow it is cricket; at the noble game, Harrow is indeed King among schools.'

The Eton and Harrow match is one of the oldest and best-known fixtures, dating from 1800. At the second confrontation, on the old Lord's Ground, August 2, 1805, Byron played for the school and was proud that his lame foot had not prevented his acquitting himself well. In a letter two days later to his young friend, Charles David Gordon, he boasted of his achievements:

'We have played the Eton and were most confoundedly beat, however it was some comfort to me that I got 11 notches in the 1st Innings and 7 the 2nd. which was more than any of our side, except Brockman and Ipswich, could contrive to hit. After the match we dined [together, and were] extremely friendly, not a single [discordant word] was uttered by either party. To be sure, we were most of us *rather* drunk, and went together to the Haymarket Theatre where we kicked up a row, as you may suppose when so many Harrovians and Etonians met at one place. I was one of seven in a single Hackney Coach, 4 Eton and 3 Harrow fellows, we all got into the same box, the consequence was that such a devil of a noise arose that none of our neighbours could hear a word of the drama, at which, not being *highly delighted*, they began to quarrel with us, and we nearly came to a *battle royal*. How I got home after the play God knows. I hardly recollect, as my brain was so much confused by the heat, the row, and the wine I drank, that I could not remember in the morning how the deuce I found my way to bed.'[3]

Harrow's sad defeat on this occasion was underlined by an epigram sent from Eton:

> *Adventurous 'boys' of Harrow School,*
> *Of cricket you've no knowledge!*
> *Ye played not cricket, but the fool*
> *With men of Eton college!*

Since 1818 the annual two-day event has been played at Lord's, except during the two world wars. Eton set an unbroken record by winning every match from 1819 to 1838 (which would seem to dispose of Harrow's kingly claim). In the eighteen-seventies the carriages stood six or more deep around the pitch and 25,000 supporters were present. At a great Eton victory in 1910 a Cabinet minister wept, laughing and dancing on a Harrovian flag, and portly citizens shouted the news down Bond Street.

It was in the summer of 1955, on the eve of John's entering Harrow, that I attended my first and only Eton and Harrow match as the guest of an Old Etonian. I found to my dismay that my host possessed a superb wheeled carriage which was parked with many others on the perimeter of the ground. It was a magnificent vehicle with polished brass lamps, and the dark ebony-type wood-work shone richly in the sun. Behind stood the maroon Rolls Royce, which on this occasion demurely took second place. I seemed to be the only hatless woman there. The ladies had stepped straight out of a couturier's salon, wearing jewellery in perfect taste, and the men had donned morning suits and top hats. Harrow boys, dressed in their tails, sported blue cornflowers in their buttonholes. It was a wedding gathering rather than a school-boys' cricket match.

Vast wicker picnic baskets appeared, and the fare was laid on hand-embroidered tablecloths. There was caviare and cham-pagne, smoked salmon and trout, ham carved off the bone, petits fours and marrons glacés. Butlers served the drinks on silver trays, cut glass sparkled in the sun. Well-trained maids scuttled in the background, in black dresses and small, white-laced, dainty aprons. The Etonians and Harrovians were trying to outdo each

131

other in their hospitality and practised casualness. It was the display of wealth that worried me. There must have been some boys who felt that the 'show' was outrageous. Everyone was on friendly Christian name terms: it was a Society get-together. The gathering was inter-related, its members spoke the same language, and with the same accent. What, I wondered, would the happy carefree village cricket team think if they were suddenly transported to this event – could they believe it was really the same game in progress? It was a far cry from the modest functions I attended during my schooldays in Scotland.

There were about 14,000 spectators at that match in 1955, but within twenty years the attendance had dropped to 2,500; and the last traditional two-day match was played at Lord's in 1981, though a one-day match there is still on the fixture list.

The Very Rev. Dr Edward Carpenter, now Dean of West-minster Abbey, told me that he had once been a curate at St Mary's, Harrow, the parish church of The Hill. On a summer's day in 1940 he was walking up The Hill with his rector and superior, the Rev. Edgar Stogden, who had once given him striking advice: 'Never preach a sermon on politics or religion. Such subjects are far too controversial for the pulpit.' France had fallen; young men and women were being conscripted into the Armed Forces and dying in their thousands to defend Britain from Nazi invasion: food was rationed, so was petrol, and we all clutched the coupon books without which we could not buy clothing and shoes: German bombers were making havoc of London, eleven miles distant: Western civilisation was heading for destruction. Rector and curate walked up towards St Mary's discussing the grim events which they had just heard on the one o'clock news. Their way took them past Bill Yard (as School Yard is commonly known), going towards Old Schools, and Edward noticed a vast number of boys standing in total silence, listening reverently. He commented on this to the rector, who silenced him – 'Ssh,' he told the young curate. 'A Harrow boy is being awarded his flannels.'

An Harrovian who had won his flannels was instantly recog-nised by the speckled straw hat he wore. His status among masters and boys alike was such that according to A. C. M. Croome, he probably never possessed so much power again. The game's im-portance as an index to a man's worth, may be judged by the number of cricketing phrases which have passed into common

132

speech: 'It isn't cricket'; 'Keep a straight bat'; 'Play the game'. *Baxter's Second Innings*, a Victorian bestseller published in 1892, was written by the Free Church evolutionist, Henry Drummond. Its hero, a diffident young boy by the name of Baxter, gets some good advice from his cricket captain, beginning with a warning against the demon fast bowler, 'Temptation':

'Tim who?' said the boy.
'Temptation,' repeated the Captain.
'Oh,' said the boy. 'I hope you are not going to be religious. I thought we were talking about games.'
'So we are,' replied the Captain cheerily. 'We are talking about the game of life . . . life is simply a cricket match – with Temptation as the Bowler.'[11]

It is easy to smile at this narrow and muscular Christianity, but perhaps the time has come once again to acknowledge its virtues rather than its shortcomings.

Games have long been seen as an excellent means of keeping boys out of trouble. Describing the great Dr Arnold, Head Master of Rugby 1828–42, David Newsome says in *Godliness and Good Learning* (1961) that he believed that 'boys should be left to choose their own forms of recreation in their out-of-school hours, and it was better that the high-spirited "bloods" should indulge their love of dangerous living in playing football rather than worrying the neighbourhood with poaching and rowdyism'. No doubt the residents of Harrow benefited in their turn when the school acquired, in 1905, 254 acres of land ideally suited to games. Inaugurated by Edward VII and Queen Alexandra, the playing-fields stretch from the gardens of the boarding-houses down to the London Road (on the other side of which is Ducker).

Since its founding in 1853, the Philathletic Club has been in charge of games administration. It is an exclusive establishment, electing its own members, though the names of those proposed for election are submitted to the Head Master by the Head of School, as *ex officio* president. The number of members of 'the Phil' should not exceed thirty, and the prestige of being elected far surpasses becoming a monitor. These young men encourage and organise games throughout the school; they discuss appointments to team captaincies with the masters in charge; and 'they are concerned to maintain in the school good standards of deportment and dress'.

Since Harrow's early days, prizes have been given for 'leaping and running and other athletic exercises'. Athletes spend many hours training for the House cups. Young masters are on parade by the asphalt running-track, stop-watches in hand, anxiously urging, advising, timing, supervising the hand-over of the baton in relay races. I remember one housemaster who made rash promises of champagne if his House proved victorious in the finals.

There is no single Sports Day at Harrow. Instead, the athletic competitions are held on a series of afternoons and evenings at the end of the Spring Term. In my memory they were always days of brilliant sun and cool breeze, when the school glowed in full sunlight, and the majestic oaks, chestnuts and elms exuded stability and peace. The great trees have seen many a generation come and go, and there are those, still unborn, who will be drawn under their spell of wonder.

I love the mystique of athletics – the gracefulness unique to the sport. Even the limbering-up period emphasises the beauty of well-formed and healthy bodies.

During our time at Harrow, there was a boy who was a 'natural' at games. A superb runner, he circled the track with no sign of effort, seeming to glide past us, his long legs striding over the ground. He could have modelled for Leonardo da Vinci. His name was Michael O'Connor.

The last weeks of the Spring Term were the time of year I enjoyed most. I would go from the pole-vaulting to the long-distance running, from the javelins to the hurdles. Every year records would be broken. Surely there will come a time when sprinters will fail to run faster, javelin-throwers fail to throw further, pole-vaulters fail to soar higher? What are the limits to physical prowess?

Rugby football is the official game played in the Christmas Term. The masters considered it a privilege – rather than a burden – to train the First XV. John was in charge for our last five years at Harrow, and I had to suffer the anger of housemasters whose boys were dropped from the team or failed to obtain a place. Many is the time I sat with the telephone in my hand, listening to a furious senior master criticising the selection. One particular housemaster would telephone each week, immediately after the team was announced. I became wise to the regularity of these calls, and would have a book to hand which I could read during the lengthy diatribes. Apart from this weekly explosion, he was very pleasant to me. Without me as scapegoat, he might have abused the boys, for he knew as well as I did that although John was the master in charge, the final decision lay on the shoulders of the Captain who had in turn been appointed by 'the Phil'; he could find himself in a difficult position, wishing to put a close friend in the team – or another member of his House. Much depended on the tact and gentle persuasion of the master in charge.

When John first arrived at Harrow, he was rather over-enthusiastic, and I well remember how deflated he was when he took the Second XV to Stowe for a match. John asked the coach driver to stop at the perimeter of Stowe's grounds, and instructed the boys to get out.

'I want you all to limber up after the long journey. We'll alternate press-ups and short sprints until we reach the top of the drive. I'll lead the way.'

Off he went, running his hundred-yards sprint, and was just completing his press-ups when he realised that he was entirely on his own. He reluctantly returned down the drive and found the boys sitting on the grass enjoying the fresh air. They had chosen this way of impressing on John the fact that they were not a crowd of preparatory-school boys straight out of the nursery. It was a lesson well learnt.

One year I decided to accompany the First XV to a school some distance south of London. The master in charge of rugger was also a housemaster, and had invited us to lunch before the match. His wife was artistic, and they had a large and magnificent garden. There were masses of flowers in every room, and an excellent meal had been laid on in their private dining-room. We had not met the couple before and were disconcerted when every remark we made was answered by a monosyllable. This continued throughout the meal. John and I found that we were conducting a conversation between ourselves. We tried to remember jokes to bridge the silences, but however funny the story, it received a cold response without even a flicker of a smile. As we rose with relief from the dining-table, the wife said to me: 'I really don't know how you can joke before a school match. We're both so tense that we can't relax until the game is finished.'

After that I stood on the touchline praying that we should lose the match, as I could not bear the thought of being confronted by a depressed couple over a silent and tearful tea. My prayers were not answered, Harrow won comfortably – but we had an excellent tea, for the housemaster and his wife were now totally at ease, and were able to accept defeat gracefully.

At another school the master in charge of rugger became so fraught that his wife had to leave the house during the rugger season. The boys were in a very difficult situation. Every match was preceded by a long lecture on the style of play practised by the members of the opposing team. Typewritten notes appeared on the games notice-board, stating which variety of tactics each player should use. It became a nightmare for the boys. On one occasion, this school had a match at Harrow. It was a good game, and Harrow won by a single point. Both teams enjoyed themselves, but the master in charge of the visiting XV turned on his heel and refused to speak to them. He would not come to my house for tea, nor could he be found when the coach was ready to leave. The boys returned to their school unsupervised, dropping off at a pub, and arriving back – understandably – the worse for wear. The master's immaturity had turned a success into a failure.

Harrow was fortunate enough to have Stephen R. Smith who taught Geography and coached rugby. He was capped many times for England, and although fearless as a scrum-half, he remained a quiet and humble person and a rare schoolmaster, admired by his colleagues. All too soon, Stephen, his wife and young family left Harrow for Calcutta where he became a missionary. He is now the Head Master of Caterham School in Surrey.

To Harrow's great good fortune, Air Chief Marshal Sir Augustus Walker, GCB, CBE, came to referee occasional matches for the First XV: a remarkable man who had been a great games player in his school days, rugby was one of his particular joys. He was captain of RAF rugby from 1936–39, and in 1939 he played for England. During the War he was awarded the DSO and DFC for bravery. He suffered the loss of his right arm, and such serious facial injuries that his nose had to be remade by plastic surgery; but he was undaunted – 'Much worse to lose a leg' – and once out of hospital decided that if he could not fulfil his rugby ambitions as an international player, he would train as an international referee. It was not beneath him to be at Cardiff Arms Park one week, and the humbler fields of Harrow the next.

We always asked the referee to lunch at our home before the match. The first time that Gus came, we had lunch, and after coffee he went to change into his rugger clothes. He returned to the sitting-room carrying his spotless boots. 'Please, John, will you help me with these, I can do most things, but I cannot manage to tie my laces.' John knelt down and spent several minutes threading and tying the laces. Gus looked up at me and smiled. Up he got, and took a few steps. The laces slipped and the boots came loose. I cannot repeat his comment here, but it was to the effect that if anyone could tie laces worse than John, he had yet to meet them. Gus was an example to us all. Life was never dull for him.

The Harrow fields would make good rose gardens – for roses need clay. The playing-fields withstood a term's rugger, but winter's torrential rains transformed them into mud baths. Hence 'Harrow football' was devised for the Spring Term. As no other school played the game, Harrow football was confined to inter-House fixtures, or an occasional match against a team of Old Boys. After leaving Harrow in 1907, Arnold Lunn wrote:

'Edward Bowen was the Homer of Harrow football. Among the smaller boys in my house there were none who would not have preferred two hours of school work to one hour of a House game. It was not only that we loathed the game itself and the constant shouts of abuse, but we dreaded the aftermath. For those who were inefficient, or on other grounds unpopular, were frequently flogged for "slacking".'[4]

I will not try to explain the rules of Harrow football. All I remember is that a referee ran up and down with a swagger stick; that on occasions a boy catching the ball would shout 'Yards!' at the top of his voice; and that the aim was to 'get a base'. To me Harrow football was an anticlimax after a good rugger season. Several school songs are dedicated to the game. They are sung lustily, for the tunes are good, which is more than can be said for the game itself. It has never been truly popular, but still it lingers on, and has to be tolerated for one term each year.

In the past, all members of the First Cricket XI, the First Harrow Football XI and the First Rugger XV were immediately termed 'bloods' – dandies, men of fashion, entitled to flaunt a fancy waistcoat regardless of age or seniority – and had the right to become members of 'the Phil'. Asquith said: 'A blood strolling down the middle of the road with that "tranquil consciousness of effortless superiority" could be described as a true essence of "The Club" manner.'

In the mid-nineteen-sixties a Head of School – an excellent games player, and a student of considerable intellect – decided that members of the First Harrow Football XI should lose this automatic right. There was strong opposition at the time, and the master in charge of Harrow football resigned on the spot. After trying to manage by himself for two weeks, the Head of School went to the Head Master's study and said: 'I don't know what the solution is.' The Head Master, characteristically warming his coat tails in front of the fire, smiled and nodded, and in his wisdom said: 'If there is no obvious solution, do nothing.' The situation was duly resolved.

Harrovians tell me that the game of squash racquets, one of the most popular today, originated at Harrow in the nineteenth century when boys would 'knock up a ball on any spare piece of wall'. A haphazard jumble of courts was constructed for each House, including windows, doors and drainpipes – which must have made the game more difficult and exciting. Not until 1864 were the first racquets courts built.

Eton fives was introduced to Harrow by a master who had previously taught there. Neither as well-known nor as energetic as squash, it is played with a padded glove instead of a racquet. It is a slower game than squash, perhaps more suitable for the middle-aged.

Harrow now boasts excellent squash courts, fives courts and racquets courts, and a nine-hole golf course overlooks the farm. The only facility missing is a football stadium!

Another change since our day is the new central dining-hall, beautifully designed, ideally situated, and endowed with all the latest kitchen equipment. This caters for the whole school, and I understand the food is consistently excellent. In our time at Harrow each House catered for itself, and I remember Joan Morgan at 'Moreton's' making breakfast, lunch and dinner for seventy boys, when the kitchen staff left suddenly (a 'good' dress hung behind the kitchen door so that she could change if parents arrived unexpectedly). Food played an important part in the life of a Harrow boy – the same is true of any boarding-school – and before the new central dining-hall was built, boys used to spend much of their time and money at 'The Hill'. This was their social centre where they could obtain every delicacy any boy could wish for. The First XI would be found here, minutes before a match, guzzling eggs, sausages and bacon under the benign eye of Jim Craig, manager of 'The Hill', and a friend to them all. Here, too, after a match, visiting schools would be entertained.

* * *

The playing-fields of Harrow were used for more than just sport. One activity, taken very seriously by some, was the Cadet Corps.

The Harrow School Corps began as a Volunteer Corps in 1859, a time when national relationships in Europe were suffering considerable strain. At first an unpopular innovation, it later became part of the secular trinity – Games, Corps and Empire; it owed its success to the fact that the 'bloods' eventually joined it, thereby guaranteeing its prestige. From 1908 until the Second World War it was known as the Officers' Training Corps. In 1939 it merged with other public-school corps, as the Junior Training Corps; and after the War was formally named the Combined Cadet Force.

Shooting proficiency was important, and to encourage this, House matches were arranged. In the early days of Harrow's existence, John Lyon made it compulsory that 'every Harrow boy shall bring to school a bow and shafts to practise archery' on Sundays 'after Mass'. From 1684 to 1771 there was an annual match when boys competed for a silver arrow. It was a great event; each boy was allowed ten shots and a 'bull' was saluted by French horns. The day ended with 'The Silver Arrow Ball'. A few of the silver arrows survive and are on display. The name is still used for the shooting-match, although the silver arrow has become a leaden bullet. Harrow excelled at Bisley, and frequently won the public-school shooting-match, together with the Spencer Cup which was awarded for the best individual marksmanship.

I can still remember my sadness when I first saw John dressed in Army officer's uniform, and the shudder of horror I felt when I watched the Corps in training. Boys were lined up in long queues, and about fifty yards in front of them were two straw dummies attached to poles stuck in the ground, with limbs dangling, and heads loosely leaning forward. Each boy in turn charged towards these imitation humans, and with a blood-curdling yell thrust his bayonet into the area of the stomach, wrenched out the weapon, and ran back to the end of the line. The Commanding Officer was in a frenzy of emotion, shouting: 'In out, on guard!' 'Well done, boy, you've got him in the guts!' 'He won't die from that – I said "kill him, kill him"!' What pent-up feelings can be released here – or can this 'game', I wonder, sicken the young adult mind?

At the firing-range, there were further human 'bodies' on view, this time painted on board. The heart was marked with a diagram, and the bullets which reached the bull's-eye scored full marks for certain death.

In the nineteen-fifties the Harrow Cadet Corps was compulsory for all boys, although they could opt for the Army, Navy or Air Force section. The Commanding Officer, a Territorial, looked the part with his military moustache and a grey streak of hair. He was keen – over-keen at times – and worried constantly how to make the training-sessions realistic and 'correct'. Mock battles were staged with smoke bombs and blanks. The new masters, fresh from university, were expected to 'volunteer' to train the Corps. Most had completed the two years of compulsory National Service, and so knew the drill. It was no hardship for those who had not been on active service, but men who had experienced the horrors of real battle must have found it difficult to play killing games.

Every year a General Inspection was taken by a high-ranking officer of one of the three Services, each being represented in turn. It took weeks to organise. The school lake made an ideal place for the assault course. The trees creaked under the weight of boys pulling themselves across the water, or scrambling into the topmost branches which could be used as observation posts. Many fell, and had to clamber up the muddy banks or resort to a rope bridge to safety. The long period of training culminated on the parade ground, with ranks of clean-shaven cadets proud of their polished buttons and shining boots marching past the high-ranking visitor as he stood to attention and took the salute, his bevy of ADCs beside him and the Commanding Officer nearby, proud of his position, yet afraid of some calamity such as a boy fainting. Not till the end of the day, when tea would be served on the terrace, could he relax and accept the inevitable congratulations from the Head Master and the inspecting dignitary.

John had had an easy life when he was conscripted and had not been on active service. He found the Wednesday training-sessions a relaxation from academic work. I found it impossible to comprehend how adults could join in this world of make-believe. I hated seeing John don his uniform. I could not understand how he could treat such a serious aspect of life in such a frivolous way. He laughed at my fears, and I became so neurotic that I had to stay in another room rather than see him in the hated uniform. One year he became particularly excited over an assault course which he had organised for the General Inspection. I was so angered by his enthusiasm that I put his Sam Browne belt in the dustbin. In his usual fashion, John left dressing until the last minute, and then

140

found his belt was missing. I confessed my guilt – he was justifiably furious. He tried to 'phone the other masters, but they were already on the parade ground. I started to see the foolish side of it – weeks of training spoilt by the loss of a belt; but though it seemed ludicrous to me, it was a Service occasion when anything less than perfection in dress and manoeuvre let down not only the person concerned, but also his unit – in this case, the school. Did he go without a belt, and get severely reprimanded by the Commanding Officer? We cannot now remember.

The summer vacation brought the Corps camps. John insisted that he only went to camp because it meant extra money. I knew better. He wanted me to think that he had to live in hardship, while I knew that had this been the case he would never have volunteered.

It is more than twenty years since those days with the Cadet Corps, and I daresay that training has changed, taking into account nuclear warfare. My twin sons volunteered to join their school Cadet Corps three years ago. They telephoned to tell me, full of excitement. 'Mother, we can learn to fly and to shoot, we can go to a training Corps camp – and we don't have to pay for it either – the taxpayer does,' they added with glee. They came home for an exeat dressed in their new Army uniforms and wearing their boots, wanting to see the expression on my face. They knew I was a pacifist. Within a year their wild enthusiasm had completely vanished and they handed in their resignations.

When I was taking a post-graduate exam at a Jesuit college, I had to write an essay on 'Whether a Christian should be a Pacifist'. Studying for this exam only confirmed my anti-war views, but I am not a conscientious objector in the full sense; I would volunteer to help relieve the suffering, and would be willing to serve with the St John's Ambulance Brigade in 'no man's land'. I am not a coward, but under no condition could I take life.

War is always horrible – never glamorous. It has been described as 'periods of intense boredom punctuated by moments of intense fright'. Yet whenever a war comes, people volunteer to fight. They do so for a variety of reasons, conscious and unconscious, good and bad, but deep down there is an inarticulate striving for right – this among the muddle and the incompetence and the sheer hell. There is a beautiful war memorial at Harrow, built in memory of the Harrovians who fell in two world wars; brave and honest men. I cannot think of a better expression of my feelings

141

than the words engraved on another war memorial, the one raised at Kohima to the dead of the Fourteenth Army:

When you go home,
Tell them of us, and say –
For your tomorrow
We gave our today.

This is what they believed. We must honour them for their belief.

Call-Over

Is it nought – our long procession,
Father, brother, friend and son,
As we step in quick succession,
Cap and pass and hurry on?
One and all
At the call,
Cap and pass and hurry on?

Here Sir! Here Sir! Here Sir! Here Sir!
On the top of Harrow Hill,
Here Sir! Here Sir! Here Sir! Here Sir!
In the windy yard at Bill.

In the Victorian era that saw the founding of the Philathletic Club, success on the playing-fields was more important to a young Harrovian, and generally to his parents too, than his being chosen as a school monitor. The same was true of the great majority of public schools. Hence, when the Head Master nominated boys as monitors, he tended to choose games players who were already members of 'the Phil' or about to be elected to it, so that they could carry out their school duties with the respect of their contemporaries. It is true that some outstanding boys who had little or no interest in or ability at sports *were* elected as monitors, and that the Head of School automatically became president of the Philathletic Club, whatever his academic or athletic preferences. When the Club was founded in 1853 by the senior boys of the fifth

143

and sixth forms, it was 'with a view of promoting among the members of the school an increased interest in games and other manly exercises'. There were to be 'pecuniary contributions', and encouragement of House matches. The optimistic declaration was, 'Those who play well, will be generally found to work well', but this view of the relationship of games to work soon proved fallacious. Nevertheless, 'the Phil' quickly became a body of enormous prestige, influence and power.

The belief that athletic achievement is more important than academic honours still exists, and applicants for academic posts may come up against it, even today. A friend of mine who was educated at Winchester and Oxford, and obtained an excellent Arts degree, decided to try for a headmastership at a well-known school. He had all the right qualifications; academically sound, he had been a good housemaster, was a member of the Church of England, and had married a respectable wife. Aware that all schools must change with the times, he had always taken an interest in the Sciences, and had studied the methods of modern language teaching.

When he arrived at his interview, he was surprised to be confronted by a rather elderly Governing Body, presided over by a bishop. Numerous purple-fronted and dog-collared men were dotted round the table. He entered the room and sat down in the chair allotted to him. There was total silence. All eyes summed him up. Eventually there was a preliminary question:

'Why do you think you would be suitable for this headmaster-ship?'

He gave his reasons. A few of the interviewers wrote notes. Another silence fell. A chair creaked. The elderly bishop turned to him and said:

'I have been looking through your curriculum vitae, but I see no mention of the games you play, although I understand you believe games are an important part of the school timetable. What games, Sir, have you played?'

'Cricket,' my friend replied cheerfully.

'Ah, good. Were you Captain of the Eleven at Winchester?'

'Oh no, I was not in *the* team.'

'Second Eleven, perhaps?'

'No – I played twice for the Fourth Eleven.'

There was an audible intake of breath. The silence was intense.

144

The eyes looked anywhere but at the applicant. The bishop swallowed.

'Twice for the Fourth Eleven?' he asked incredulously. He pondered, and a thought came to him. Raising his head, he continued:

'Ah, but you are still young. With practice you may improve.'

The Wykehamist rose to his feet. 'Good afternoon, gentlemen – I must return to my sixth form.' My friend subsequently became headmaster of a very distinguished school. The bishops chose another applicant. He lasted four years before being asked to leave.

It is not so long since university dons interviewing applicants for places enquired about athletic prowess long before mentioning academic ability. Happily those days are past.

During the eighteen years in which he was Head Master of Harrow, 1953–71, Dr James built up a new sense of pride in academic achievement. Harrow's success in the Oxford and Cambridge entrance examinations improved dramatically, and it is fair to say that under his influence Harrow in the nineteen-sixties could lay some claim to being one of the 'academic' schools while still achieving a good comprehensive education for all. His Victorian predecessors would have shaken their heads over such a profound change in the climate of opinion. When the young Walter Sichel succeeded in the Balliol scholarship examination in 1872, he was astonished to find himself being clapped down the steps of Old Schools at Call-over. He could recall no other occasion when the school had accorded such an honour for anything but success in games and athletics. Lionel Ford, Head Master 1910–25, traced this attitude to its source when he said, 'The parents are more obsessed with games than their sons.' In his own day the majority of boys, even the clever ones, were bored by their lessons. Nor is it surprising. Augustus Hare (Harrow, 1847–48) said in *The Story of My Life* (1896) that he 'never learnt anything useful . . . hours and hours were wasted daily on useless Latin verses, with sickening monotony'. In 1890 another Harrow Head Master, J. A. C. Welldon (1885–98), told the Headmasters' Conference how painful it was to read the biographies of men who had found their years at school intellectually wasteful 'because their attention was forcibly directed to subjects for which they had no aptitude'.

Dr James wrote few, if any, papers on the ideals of headmastership, and rarely spoke on the matter. However, he had a great influence on the younger masters, and was generous in helping those who decided to apply for headmasterships of their own. My gratitude for our years at Harrow is largely due to the kindness we experienced from him and from colleagues whom I learned to respect. He had a good senior staff to encourage and support him in the struggle to upgrade Harrow's intellectual standards. Among them were Len Walton, the Head of Modern Languages; three classicists, E. V. C. Plumptre (otherwise known as 'Plum'), Ronald Watkins and Mark Warman; and two mathematicians, John Morgan and Kenneth Snell. These senior men were the backbone of the Common Room. A housemaster has his fellow housemasters to turn to for support and advice – a headmaster has to 'go it alone', and be answerable to all. The position is a lonely one. I remember the headmaster of a Benedictine school saying to me: 'When I was a housemaster, I thought I knew all the answers to running a school, and I criticised the headmaster; now that I am a headmaster, I know better. I had no idea of the extent of the problems – or the variety of them – which were ultimately the responsibility of the Head.'

I remember Harrow as a school of great potential. We were fortunate to have Jimmy James as Head Master – he was, unusually in this profession, a humble man, and moreover a very wise one. He trusted his masters, respected their privacy, yet demanded high standards. His responsibilities were great. The Public Schools Calendar for 1866 summed up the Harrow headmastership as follows: 'It has been the practice of the Governors to leave the administration of the school entirely in the hands of the Head Master, who is completely unshackled by any superior administrative authority, and consequently it is open to him, and must therefore be his duty, to make such changes from time to time as may appear to him at once desirable in themselves and opportune in respect of circumstances. He appoints all the Assistant Masters, gives permission to open Boarding-Houses, and is responsible for the financial arrangements of the School.' During our own time at the school, Jimmy James was at the peak of his career.

A shy man, Jimmy James disliked attending social functions outside the school. If persuaded to accept, he would be found in the least crowded corner, near to the door so that he could slip away unobtrusively. Yet on his home ground he was an excellent host. He gave his full support to the fund-raising functions which we held each year. The largest of these was the Christmas Charity Fête, organised by the school with help from the other residents of

146

The Hill. This provided useful money for charity, but it was also a wonderful opportunity for all the residents of The Hill to feel that they were part of one community. Bobbie James was the instigator of these events. She could even persuade her husband into buying raffle and tombola tickets, and much to his embarrassment he had the uncanny knack of winning on the majority of his numbers.

The occasion which must particularly tax any headmaster is Speech Day. As far as I am aware, Westminster School where John is now Head Master is the only school that does not have a Speech Day. For this I am grateful. I am not sympathetic to public functions held routinely, year after year, particularly not when they encourage 'one-upmanship' between parent and parent, or parent and boys. A friend of mine was until recently headmaster of a well-known school with an annual Speech Day in the usual style. No building in the school was large enough to accommodate the parents and all the boys, let alone their sisters and their cousins and their aunts, so the school hired an extremely expensive marquee for speeches and prize-giving. There were so many parents that the Head Master could not do more than give each a quick handshake. The usual exhibitions of work in the Sciences and the Arts were dotted about the buildings, but with such a throng of people it was impossible to appreciate the excellence of the work on show. The boys gave gymnastic displays, and entertained their visitors in the music schools with a choice of classical, 'pop', steel or brass bands. Housemasters made vain attempts to have quiet, relaxed conversations with parents, but there were always queues of others building up to await their turn, and they had to shout to make themselves heard over the babble of voices during House tea; privacy was impossible, and the whole day seemed a complete and unjustifiable waste of time.

The Head Master therefore wrote to the parents to say that he thought it would be far more valuable to have smaller gatherings, when parents would have ample opportunity to see the masters and housemasters, and could be brought up to date with their son's academic career. He also told the firm which usually supplied the marquee that he was cancelling the order for the following year, and he mentioned the expense as one reason for doing so.

There was an outcry. Those parents who replied did so in anger. Speech Day was a tradition. No matter what the battle for survival in the scrum of people, it was worth the effort; no matter what the charge for the marquee, it was worth the cost. Was it, I wonder, the parents of the prize-winners who expressed their views so adamantly? The following year Speech Day was again on the calendar. The marquee was booked but this time the firm offered it at half the previous cost.

A state-school headmaster told me that he couldn't understand how the parents of Westminster's boys could allow us to survive without a Speech Day. 'I hate the day,' he said. 'I have to spend hours on my speech, and few listen to it, apart from the governors sitting on the platform beside me – and sometimes they're so old they fall asleep. I tried to stop it once, and wrote to the county educational authorities, but they would not even consider my plea. I was told that young Johnnie and Annie had to have their prizes, and that the public must be present to see the Government's generosity to the children.'

At Westminster, the boys used to crowd 'Up School' for the final assembly of the academic year, on the last day of the Summer (Election) Term. Now even that has changed, and a prize-winner receives his reward in a private interview with the Head Master in Ashburnham drawing-room.

Harrow was a school which took its Speech Day seriously. Housemasters had special invitations printed, inviting the families of boys to spend the day at the school. Assistant masters like John were also invited to join various Houses, and would jokingly vie with each other over the number of invitations each could ostentatiously place on the mantelpiece of his study.

The boys normally attended Early Morning School at 7.30 a.m., but on Speech Day they were allowed to walk down to Ducker instead to have an early dip. Few availed themselves of this, instead they took advantage of an extra 'lie-in' until the dew on the grass dried in the morning sun. Speech Day was always in the summer, and out of the eleven years we were at the school I remember only one when the weather was unkind to us.

Parents started to arrive at about ten o'clock, driving up in a magnificent array of cars, polished to a high showroom gloss, and ranging from shooting-brakes (some carrying an occasional black retriever) to a mauve Mercedes, a gold-plated, star-spangled Daimler, and one or two privately-owned London taxis. They lined The Hill and were crowded into the House grounds. The boys were immaculately dressed in their tails, each with a buttonhole in his lapel to acknowledge the occasion.

148

At about eleven o'clock Dr Jimmy James would be seen in cap and gown walking over to Bill Yard for Call-over. This was a daily event, normally taken by other masters, but on Speech Day, with parents watching, the Head Master had to preside. He stood on the steps that went up to Old Schools, Custos behind him, the duty monitors ready to report, and the boys waiting in a long single file in the courtyard. As the clock struck the hour, the official ceremony of Call-over commenced in 'Bill order'. Each boy passed in front of the Head Master as his name was read out, raised his boater, and said, 'Here, Sir.'

A band from one of the smarter Regiments, brought by coach, would start to play, and the music would continue for many an hour on the terrace below the Library and the Chapel – a beautiful place, with views across the countryside to the haze of London.

After Call-over, boys were free to wander with their parents. Ducker was an attraction, and the Ducks and Ducklings races would be held there – races for the senior and junior boys (adequately clothed). The families would line the pool, and throng onto the bridge for a better viewpoint. It was an elegant scene – the magnificently-situated pool gracefully curving into the distance, tall trees giving welcome shade, well-mown lawns, roses in full bloom, the mingled scents of freshly-cut grass and roses and the honeysuckle that grew over the changing-sheds. The pale dresses of the ladies flickered in the breeze, their picture hats and sunshades had the charm of a Victorian print: it was another world.

At lunchtime the King's Head Hotel on The Hill would be full to overflowing with Harrovians. Delicious meals were served in the hotel garden and the indoor restaurant. For many families, though, picnic lunches in the school grounds were the order of the day. Wicker hampers would be opened, and grand picnics appeared.

Speeches and prize-giving took place after lunch. The 'speeches' were in fact recitations – often in foreign languages – and sitting attentively for an hour or so was never easy. Outside the sun was blazing, and perhaps the First XI would be playing cricket against the Harrow Wanderers – a team of Old Harrovians, some of whom had left only a term ago, while others had represented School and sometimes County half a century earlier.

After Speeches came tea. Masters and their wives made a round of Houses to which they had been invited, while the boys returned to their own Houses, together with their families, and gratefully accepted the iced coffee, China or Indian tea, cucumber sandwiches and cakes, delicious ices, strawberries ordered by the stone and cream by the gallon – there seemed to be no limits. It was a luxurious ending to a luxurious day.

Jimmy James was a man of great good sense and once gave John some of the best advice he has ever had. 'Never have a row with a colleague on paper. Speak to him face to face. If you write something down, he will read and re-read it, and the disagreement will be constantly revived.'

But Harrow had its follies too. John reminds me that when the Queen and Prince Philip came to visit the school one spring, a master commented, on the morning of the visit, that the front gardens of the Houses looked bare. So the groundsmen had to shift the daffodils from the back gardens to the front. John swears that the flowers were picked by hand, the raw stems being merely pushed into the flower-beds and window-boxes. Whatever the cause, the yellow trumpets failed to herald the Royal pair, instead they drooped to the ground in mourning. On the same visit, Prince Philip was shown round Ducker by John. Fresh paint had been used liberally on the changing-sheds, the benches, and the bridge over the centre of the pool, where visitors crowded on Speech Day. The Prince said: 'I want to walk round the other side of the bridge.' John took him round. 'Ah,' Prince Philip said, 'I see that they've painted the far side too. I often catch people out.' He never found out that it was only at John's insistence on the night before the visit that the other side had been painted.

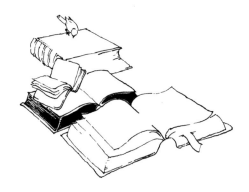

Taunton

Winston Churchill, most famous of Old Harrovians, once re-marked in his rotund style, 'Headmasters have powers at their disposal with which Prime Ministers have never yet been in-vested.' One morning in September 1965, I was reading the *Times Educational Supplement* at breakfast. I saw an advertisement for a headmaster at an Oxford school. We had not thought of John applying for such a position at this stage, but I was attracted to Oxford, and I pointed it out to him.

'No,' said John, 'too many bishops on the Governing Body – are there any other headships?'

As he had applied to Harrow 'for fun', so he now applied for his first headmastership, Taunton School. Not only did he not take the application very seriously, he had managed to convince him-self that he had cancer. We had recently bought – I forget why – a small handbook which described the early signs of this disease. John, one of the nation's hypochondriacs, read it avidly, and soon discovered that, though only thirty-four, he was riddled with tell-tale symptoms. Without my knowledge, he telephoned his doctor each night to relate the latest change in his bodily functions. He was told not to be so silly, but John knew better.

He was invited for an interview for the headmastership and arrived feeling he had nothing to lose. To the conventional questions – 'Why do you want to be a headmaster?' – he gave unconventional answers. His detachment was so refreshing that the Selection Committee appointed him without hesitation. There

151

was no chance to back out because the Governors informed Westward Television of their decision before offering the position to John.

The following August, we said our farewells to Harrow and sadly set out to face the old problems in a different setting – and some new difficulties besides.

As an assistant master, John had been concerned to some extent with discipline. As a headmaster, he was totally responsible for it. At each and every meeting with his housemasters, the word 'discipline' came up sooner or later. A brief look at the past shows that this has always been so.

John Lyon, who founded Harrow in 1571, stated that the grave offences committed by boys were those of 'swearing, lying, picking and stealing, fighting, and filthiness or wantonness of speech', and that these deserved 'moderate whipping with a rod'. A year's probation was given for the worst cases of idleness and incompetence, and if there was no improvement, the boys were expelled.

Harrow had been in existence for over 150 years when the Reverend James Cox was appointed Head Master (he had served his predecessor, Thomas Brian, as Usher and Second Master from 1722 to 1731). For the next fifteen years, 1731–46, he led a disorderly and drunken life, causing so much havoc that the school roll fell to forty pupils. In 1746 the Governors were wise enough to appoint Thomas Thackeray, who was from Eton, as Head Master in the hope of restoring Harrow's reputation. Thackeray was a friend of Frederick, Prince of Wales, and under his headmastership the number of students increased, many being sons of the British peers who supported the Hanoverians. However, in later years Thackeray became indulgent towards the boys, discipline slipped, and the school suffered. The students drank and gambled freely. Fist fights were common, and it is recorded that two Harrovians fought a duel, with swords. Young boys were bullied, kicked, beaten, and terrified when sent to spend the night hours in the churchyard among the ghosts. It is fair to add that public schools all over the country were undergoing the same problems.

In 1760 Thackeray was replaced by Robert Sumner, another Etonian, then in his early thirties. Sumner's first task was to restore discipline. As part of his campaign to persuade men of high birth to send their sons to the school, Thackeray had promised in writing that these boys would be allowed certain privileges, such as not being present at 'Bill' – the roll-call to check that all the boys were at school for lessons. To the great anger of some of the parents, Sumner refused to allow this favouritism to continue. He was firm-handed, an excellent teacher and a great orator. He particularly encouraged the use of Houses as an integral part of school life rather than merely as places where the boys slept and ate. He stimulated the school's intellectual life – and arranged, too, a dancing-school for the less academic.

Among Sumner's pupils was Richard Brinsley Sheridan (Harrow, 1762–68), later to be a great dramatist and vigorous politician. The young Sheridan became attached to the beautiful and gifted Elizabeth Ann Linley, daughter of the composer Thomas Linley and prima donna at his concerts. A lovely girl of sixteen, she had many suitors, including a certain Major Matthews who forced his attentions on her with such determination that in March 1772 she fled abroad to escape him. It was Sheridan who escorted her to France and there installed her in a convent, first going through a secret marriage with her near Calais; he then returned to England and fought two duels with Major Matthews. A year later he and Elizabeth Ann were married for the second time – this time openly; and in January 1775 his first comedy, *The Rivals*, was staged at Drury Lane. In 1781 the Sheridans returned to Harrow, to live at 'The Grove', now a flourishing House.

In 1771 Sumner died suddenly, aged forty-one. He had only been at Harrow for a decade, but in that time the number of students had risen to 232. When the Governors offered the vacant headmastership to Dr Benjamin Heath, from Eton, there was an outcry among the boys who had hoped that a popular Harrow master would be chosen; their fury was such that they destroyed a carriage belonging to one of the Governors. However, Heath was another disciplinarian, he promptly took control, and under his rule (1771–85) the school flourished. He was emulated by his great friend and successor, Dr Joseph Drury, Head Master from 1785 to 1805, during whose period Harrow educated five future Prime Ministers – Peel, Palmerston, Aberdeen, Goderich (first Earl of Ripon) and Spencer Perceval – and the poet Byron besides.

In 1805, when Byron was in his last year as a student, Dr Drury retired. The boys had expected Drury's very popular nephew to be appointed Head Master, and when the Governors instead chose Dr George Butler, there was an outcry. Byron wrote satires on the new Head and circulated them among his contemporaries. Tension grew to such a pitch that the boys devised a plan to blow up the Head Master and laid a trail of gunpowder in the cellar under Old Schools though they eventually decided against firing it when they realised that the explosion would not only blow up Butler, but would also destroy the signatures carefully carved on the walls by previous Harrovians, Byron's being one of the largest and most flamboyant of them all. None the less, the rebellion grew increasingly serious. Monitors resigned: Peachey's key was stolen forcibly (he was the then Custodian): the birch cupboard was broken open: the Head Master's chair was badly damaged – and then burnt: a strike was proclaimed, the London Road blockaded, and all means of communication between the school and the outside world were stopped.

What would be a headmaster's reaction today? Butler was a man who abhorred bullying in any form, but he had no intention of putting up with such a situation. He immediately expelled the ringleaders and quelled the mutiny. He acted with such speed and efficiency that he was congratulated by George III for his handling of the riot.

★   ★   ★

John and I were both rather young when we went to Taunton School in Somerset – and, what was worse, we looked younger than our years. When we were introduced at Taunton, people asked if John and I were the new Head Master's son and daughter-in-law; much the same thing happened when we moved to Westminster four years later.

Taunton, primarily a boys' boarding-school, was a male-dominated establishment. On my first Sunday there, I telephoned the Deputy Head – the eminent biologist Dr Ernest Neal – to ask the time of the Chapel service. He told me, but 'could he ask why I wanted to know'. I replied that I wanted to make my plans so as to be free to go.

'Women don't go to Chapel – it isn't traditional,' he said.

'Well, I'm going tonight,' I replied, fearing that if I decided to 'chicken out' then, I would never have the courage to try again.

'Oh good,' he exclaimed, 'my wife will be delighted to join you. She has been waiting many years to do this.'

Betty Neal and I walked into Chapel with our husbands to the amazement of boys and staff. Afterwards, I wrote round to the

154

masters' wives (there were about thirty, I think), saying that I hoped they would feel free to come to Sunday Chapel if they so wished. I had only two replies and both said that they saw no need for change in an all-male establishment; but by the time we left, four years later, it was common to see women at services. It was not only the wives who clung to the old traditions. A Governor was so incensed when my husband suggested, one Easter, that the school orchestra should give their performance of Mozart's Requiem Mass in the chapel instead of the concert hall, that he resigned from the Governing Body.

I found that being married to a headmaster was a lonely, segregated position. I had much preferred being an assistant master's wife, though other wives, more ambitious, might feel differently. On one occasion at Taunton I had to attend a staff Christmas party without John. He was in bed with 'flu, and had insisted that I should 'make an appearance', but I intended to leave early, using his sickness as my excuse. I stayed for about an hour, enjoyed an excellent buffet supper, at which many of the staff were present, and said my farewells to my hosts at the front door. Suddenly realising that I had left my handbag in the house, I re-opened the door and went into the dining-room just in time to hear my host say in a loud voice: 'All right everyone, you can relax and enjoy yourselves now, she's left safely.' It was too late to retrace my steps. I walked to the far end of the now silent room to pick up my bag, wished the staff a Merry Christmas, and quickly left the premises.

My sense of isolation at Taunton was accentuated by the fact that the previous headmaster had been a bachelor and there were few women in the school environment. Boys were said to be 'slushing' if they spoke to a master: there was no word strong enough to call them if they dared speak to a woman. A far cry from Harrow! I called at the Sanatorium and asked if the female staff would try to walk through the corridors of the main school building when the bell rang for Break and again at the end of Morning School, in order to say 'Good morning' to the boys. I think they persevered for a few days, then quietly abandoned the idea. It was too revolutionary.

We had been at Taunton for two terms before one of the boys spoke to me. I was with my children watching a cricket match on a magnificent summer's day. A Nigerian boy passed by and remarked on the weather. 'Yes, Tom,' I replied. 'This is the best day

I have had since I came to Somerset.' He looked a bit bewildered at my enthusiasm, so I added, 'You're the first boy who has spoken to me.'

The spell was broken, and the children and I were accepted by the boys from then on.

The following day, John asked me to lunch with the boys in the communal dining-room. I gleefully accepted, and he said that he would make it a weekly routine. He did not tell me at the time that I was going to face this ordeal on my own; instead he waited until I reached the door into the dining-room before saying, 'It will emphasise your presence if I don't come in with you – you must go through with this'; he deposited me at the doorway and disappeared down the passage, leaving me to walk through two lines of masters to the table at which the prefects were sitting. I was alone and terrified, and very aware of the strange glances from the masters' table, but I survived. The boys were wonderful, and after that regularly placed a small bunch of flowers from the school garden on the table allocated to me.

Whenever a new headmaster is appointed to a school, there are changes to be made. Some are welcomed, others resented. Discipline has to be tightened in some areas, slackened in others. Some of the masters may be made redundant, some of the 'gang leaders' among the boys expelled: it is a difficult time, and the burden is enormous. The 'Head' is the father-figure and has to be seen as such, both by the pupils and by the staff – though the latter might never admit it. No assistant master or housemaster can ever experience the thousand and one problems which the Head Master has to shoulder. It is he who has to adjudicate in the various feuds between staff and staff, boys and boys, staff and boys. He oversees the Staff Common Room, yet cannot mingle there freely. He is always the outsider. Although parents usually approach their son's housemaster first with any problem, it is the Head Master who is, and must be, the ultimate authority. 'The buck stops here,' as Harry Truman said. He has to be the one secure figure who is discreet at all times, and always to be relied upon for an honest judgment. He has to support his colleagues, even when he is hoping that they will soon apply for jobs in other schools. He has to trust his senior boys to help with discipline, even when he knows that their housemaster may be framing the rules unwisely. I remember a distraught group of boys who came round to our house one evening, protesting against the 'puerile disciplinary rules which our housemaster insists on'.

'The House is so tense,' they said, 'it would only take a desk lid banging down to make the boys explode.' After the group had gone, John said to me, 'I wish they had dropped *all* the desk lids. An explosion is just what that housemaster needs. He is far too petty, and he needs to be taught a lesson.'

The period we spent at Taunton coincided with the 'depression' in the public schools. Discipline in general was poor, and because the grammar schools were selective and successful, many parents who might otherwise have chosen a public-school education for their children opted to send them to these excellent establishments, which had the additional advantage of being free, or at least very much less expensive. Public-school headmasters looked at their advance lists, noted that there were few – if any – boys being entered, and immediately got in touch with local prep-school headmasters. We ourselves spent many days visiting prep schools, meeting prospective parents, and trying to induce them to enter their sons for Taunton. Until this time it had been necessary to put a child's name down for public school at birth, so great was the demand, yet here we were actually touting for custom. This was a country-wide phenomenon, not just in our area.

On one occasion we went to a nearby school where Taunton was due to play a rugger match. We stopped at the front gates and asked a group of about twenty boys where the playing-fields were: not one of them understood what we were saying, for none could speak English. Some headmasters had become so anxious that they had decided to take the easy way out and fill the empty places with boys from overseas. Foreign parents were eager to send their sons – half a dozen or so letters arrived every day requesting boarding-places for boys from Middle Eastern countries, or even the Far East. So headmasters accepted them, but made little or no effort to help them adjust once they arrived: even in their second year in England, they still had little idea of how to communicate with their British contemporaries. Some schools specialised in accepting boys belonging to certain cultures, not because they intended to appoint a particular master to take charge of their education, but rather to create a group or 'hive' environment into which these boys would settle comfortably, sparing themselves and the school any adjustment difficulties.

Many public schools now faced the dilemma that in order to

comply with educational standards they must provide more – and expensive – facilities, and yet they could not afford to do so because their waiting-lists were so meagre. A number of schools simply closed down. Others decided to accept girls as boarders – some in the sixth form only, others taking girls from the age of eleven or thirteen. These schemes resulted in some haphazard and emergency accommodation in the early years, but gradually they have stabilised, and the financial situation has become stronger. Mixed-boarding has now been established, and has benefited both staff and pupils. Six years after our arrival at Taunton, but sadly not until two years after we had moved on to Westminster, the nearby girls' school amalgamated with the boys', and although, no doubt, previous Governors turned in their graves, the amalgamation has been a great success.

14

Westminster

We were at Taunton for four years before moving to Westminster. I was with John when he was offered this headmastership. I hated the thought of moving from the country so much that when I heard the 'good' news, I burst into tears – tears of sadness, not relief. I continued to hate the whole idea of uprooting our young family from the clear rural air of Somerset, even though I accepted that it was an honour for John. I kept this to myself until one day when I was talking to one of the Governors whom I knew personally; I told him my worries and can still remember his reply:

'You mustn't worry about the effect on the children's health of bringing them into Westminster. The schoolboys are so healthy that we have closed down the Sanatorium. You see,' he added, 'the river tide changes twice a day.' Unless he was trying to imply that the germs changed with the tide – or were washed away by it – this seemed the biggest *non sequitur* I had ever heard.

In August 1970 I drove the children up to London while John followed by train. Westminster School is in the precincts of the great Abbey, facing the Houses of Parliament across Old Palace Yard. I met our new housekeeper, and together we went into the Head Master's house. All the floorboards were up; there was no electricity or water; we would have to sleep in the boys' dormitories until the house was fit to live in. The study door was locked, so I climbed in through the window by way of the balcony, and to my surprise (and perhaps theirs) found the outgoing

Head Master and his wife sitting in a bare room having a picnic lunch from the top of a tea chest.

On the first day of term we moved into the house, which was still unfloored so that we had to balance on the joists. The mains cold-water tap in the kitchen did function, but we shared the rest of the water-supply with two of the boarding-houses and found that after five in the evening we had no hot water, and only the odd drop of cold. 'Your tanks have been emptied by the boys taking showers after games,' we were told.

On the third day of term we were invited out to dinner by some parents. I was filthy with the builders' dust that hung thickly in the air, my hair was lank, and I couldn't iron my evening dress as we still had no electric power. I arrived worn and ashamed at the dinner. Our host took one look at me, and said, 'You look awful.' I groped for an excuse, but then he went on, 'I insist that you and your family join us for Christmas in Switzerland.' The next day our tickets were delivered, and the hotel booking confirmed and paid in advance. A worthwhile compensation!

The house was made habitable, but still had – and has – its limitations. I do not know of any other headmaster who has to share his house – and even his front door – with sixty assistant masters, the Masters' Common Room being on the ground floor of our house. There is only one telephone number, shared by us with the school, and our front hall, opening out of the Common Room vestibule, is in continual use for tutorials. From the hall, stairs lead up to John's study on the first floor, flanked on one side by his secretary's office, and on the other by our 'private' sitting-room, which in actual fact is used as a waiting-room for parents or boys, or sometimes as a form room when John tires of teaching in his study.

Our contract allows us a housekeeper and one daily help. Over the past thirteen years we have had a rapid succession of house-keepers; most had to leave, on the verge of breakdown; one tried to commit suicide; only one lasted, and she was happy, young and beautiful, an efficient worker, and an excellent cook: a delight to be with. The boys whose studies faced her kitchen windows hung out banners saying *WE ALL LOVE LOUISE*. My younger son at the ripe age of six was madly in love with her, and saved his pocket money in order to take her out to coffee at the Italian restaurant across the road – dressed in his very best clothes. But they were all too late, for Louise was already floating on the clouds of romance, and we could only have her for that one happy year. For the last four years we have managed without a housekeeper at all, for I cannot bring myself to introduce anyone else into a situation where they are likely to be unhappy. When one housekeeper and friend, who returned three times to me, eventually gave up, we decided to count the number of people to whom we had given hospitality during a three-day period: over a hundred and forty coffees, a luncheon party for twelve, a dinner for eight, and fifty-six for sherry – plus food for a priest who was staying with us while giving Lenten Addresses. This was too much for anyone, and impossible for 'Heppie' who suffered from rheumatoid arthritis. The school is in the heart of London, a convenient place for people to stay, and there was no lack of requests for a 'bed for the night'. John at first felt obliged to offer accommodation, which meant that one of our children had to turn out of their room and sleep on the sofa: eventually the family rebelled, and said John should give up his bed instead. He made no further offers.

We had so little privacy in the house that our children insisted on having locks put on their bedroom doors. The kitchen was in constant use by everyone: the housekeeper turned out fresh-baked cakes on to a cooling-tray while she got on with something else, and found none left when she returned a few minutes later. It was always happening, and as my children were usually at school during the day they can rarely have been to blame. The telephone rang day and night, and had to be answered: if John's secretary was in another part of the school, or if it rang after office hours, the task fell to us. The house is still so accessible that there seems to be a constant stream of people wandering through it. One afternoon, I went to call my daughter Penelope to the telephone. Thinking she was having a bath after games, I banged on the bathroom door – but to no avail. Penelope often slept in the bath, so I called through the door saying that I would break it down if she did not appear. There was the sound of water splashing, the door opened, and I was confronted by an unknown man who had my bath towel wrapped round his middle.

'Please don't disturb me again,' he said, 'I haven't finished my ablutions.'

'Who are you?' I asked.

'Who are *you*?' he replied. 'I've bathed here every Tuesday and Thursday for the last three years.'

I drew in my breath and said, 'This is *my* bathroom,' and added in horror, 'And that is *my* towel you are using – it's unhygienic – how do I know you haven't got VD? Where are your clothes?'

He told me that he had undressed in one of the children's bedrooms, so I frogmarched him there with the water still dripping from his shoulders and sent him packing. He turned out to be a visiting Games master. One of the staff had given him permission to use my bathroom. John was unaware of this. When I confronted the master concerned, *he* was surprised that *I* was surprised by his action.

I remember a kindly and well-meaning headmaster's wife inviting us to dinner during our early days in Somerset: the other local headmasters and their wives were there to meet us. After the dinner, I was taken to one side by the ladies.

'There is always a lot of entertaining to be done in your position,' I was told. 'It is a great responsibility – and also expensive. We' (the speaker glanced round at the other two wives) 'work on the principle that we offer callers three types of refreshment. First, whisky, gin or brandy for those you want to impress – wealthy parents, university dons, and of course anyone from the Governing Body. Next, sherry for the ordinary folk. And last, for those who just drop in, or whom you don't expect to see again, coffee or a soft drink.' I have religiously *not* abided by this principle, and in twenty-six years of life as a schoolmaster's wife have never bought hard liquor. 'Important' guests cannot accuse me of trying to impress them.

However, I have been known – much to my husband's chagrin – to offer sherry to worried-looking boys waiting outside the study. Recently I found a boy walking up and down the landing as he waited for John to return. I had had a frustrating day in London, and when I saw his anxious look, I asked him if he was in need of a glass of sherry. He agreed readily, and John found us an hour later talking on moral theology with Schubert playing gently in the background while we drank sherry from the best cut-glass. I immediately found him a similar sedative. 'How could I be angry?' he asked me afterwards; then he added, 'But I think my intended blasting had far more effect, with the three of us meeting in such a civilised way.' Thereafter the boy was his staunch supporter.

Although I sometimes long for a little peace and privacy, I can truly say that I have never been bored. Life is never dull here. School functions alone occupy so much time and energy that there

162

is rarely a chance to rest, and living in the heart of London is much more demanding than a school deep in the country. Is it because we are so central that the numerous school and House plays and concerts, art exhibitions and other entertainments are so well attended? It is certainly a great advantage to know that we are never at a loss for expert lecturers on any academic or social subject.

But there are disadvantages too. Radio or television producers ring up John: 'We need you immediately – a car will be sent to collect you.' Newspaper editors telephone urgently requiring an article in answer to the Government's or Opposition's latest paper: it must appear in tomorrow's edition: a runner will be sent to collect it. Members of both Houses of Parliament ask for facts, or sometimes for a full written speech. Even the Palace may request an opinion or advice. I could easily fill a diary with dinner invitations, but each would include giving the inevitable after-dinner speech. It is surprising that John has any time left in which to teach – but he is insistent that his first priority is to teach, and teach well, and he manages over a dozen periods a week. However much he would like to be 'one of the boys', as any other head-master he is forced to be a man apart, both because of his school responsibilities and because of the outside activities which are pressed on him by virtue of his position. Inevitably, the loneliness of his life is to some extent reflected in mine. The magazine *Punch* asked him to write about success, and he has given me permission (which I have made him sign!) to quote from his article:

'I was sceptical about the idea of success being applied to education; of all human activities only prayer affords less convincing evidence of the connection between input and effect. That good schoolmasters exist I have no doubt. Their gift (which can be developed but not I think acquired) is to be able to inspire and motivate their pupils. But there is no satisfactory measurement of their success. Exam results can be positively misleading.

But when the good schoolmaster is appointed headmaster he is pitch-forked into the public arena. Whether he likes it or not he is up against the problem of success. If he is head of an independent school the problem is more immediate; unlike his counterparts in the maintained sector he is competing in the market-place and his job security is closer to that of a football manager than of a parish priest. He needs success in some recognisable form. He may believe that his headmastership can only be judged in the perspective of history but he must reconcile himself to continuous assessment. He must also reconcile himself to the fickle and gullible nature of popular opinion. There is an element of bluff in any head-master's style, but some I have known have raised bluff to the level of art: their whole headmastership was a commedia dell'arte performance, improvised, larger than life, breezily insincere, always suggesting but never quite becoming farce. Heaven knows how they got away with it but they did and were hailed on all sides as successful headmasters.

I had not realised until I became a headmaster just how cut-throat the world of independent schools was. A polite one-upmanship characterised relations between headmasters. While not actually wishing their rivals ill, they were not unduly dismayed if it occurred. The motto of the Head-masters' Conference might have been de La Rochefoucauld's maxim: "In the misfortune of our friends is something that is not displeasing to us."

The spirit of one-upmanship was partly a reflection of the snobbery implicit in the public-school hierarchy. Some schools were acknowl-edged to be in the First Division and their headmasters were treated with a deference that in some cases they hardly merited. But competitiveness was also a reflection of the realities of the market. One school's success could be another's empty beds.

With this background it was inevitable that if one headmaster broke ranks, refused to toe the party line, attracted more than his fair share of attention in the Press and was accounted a success, his head-magisterial colleagues should feel some resentment and envy. I have been trying to think of a less provocative simile but there have been times when the reaction of other headmasters to my too frequent appearances in the media has been like that of the angry wives in a harem when one of their number appears to have cornered the affections of the sultan.

To be in the public eye has less agreeable side-effects. It exposes your family to publicity they have not sought and do not welcome. For myself I accept that if I use the Press to argue a case I cannot complain if the Press sometimes gives me publicity that I would prefer not to have. But I regret the pressure that public life has placed upon my family. There is a good book to be written about public schools from the point of view of the headmaster's wife (*Tom Brown's Schooldays* without Mrs Arnold's *Memoirs* gives a very lop-sided view of Rugby). It is a difficult role and it is made more difficult if her husband is slugging it out in the public arena.

The public arena has other hazards. So deeply ingrained is the English public-school taboo against pushing oneself forward and in favour of a calculating self-effacement, that the headmaster whose name becomes too familiar is regarded as something of a cad ("brazen" was the adjective one elder statesman of the Headmasters' Conference used to describe me) and, even worse, as someone who is more concerned with his own image than the job for which he is being paid. The assumption is that a head-master who engages in public debate is not a gentleman and that he is getting his priorities wrong. A headmaster may spend all his time sitting on committees or devote two days a week to his golf or be drunk more often than not in the evenings and no one will complain. But let him write one article for the newspaper and he is labelled "ambitious"; if he writes two he is a "careerist" and anything beyond that is condemned as "publicity seeking". Even now it is not quite decent for a headmaster to be seen on television. "Didn't I see you on television?" a colleague will say accusingly as though he had spotted me slipping into a blue movie.

When I was young and uneasy, a green headmaster in the West Country, I think I did seek opportunities to be noticed by the Press. I was headmaster of a little-known school. I had none of the fashionable qualifications; I felt myself to be an outsider in the headmasterly establishment. Like the lunatic who needs to look in the mirror from time to time to reassure himself that he is still there, I needed the reassurance of publicity. It was childish and it did not work. The excitement of publishing a first book or an article or of appearing on television for the first time is brief and not repeated. After the first kick there is no other. It has been one of the blessings of what is called success that it has enabled me to grow out of this particular form of immaturity. If I write now it is because I enjoy writing and because I have something that I want to say.

Freedom from anxiety about reputation has also enabled me to reflect on what success as a headmaster really means. I came to the conclusion that celebrity neither confirms nor discredits a claim to be successful. It is just irrelevant. The real measure of a headmaster's success is more subtle and more complex. It has something to do with making the right decisions, particularly the less publicised ones. It is not the grand schemes or the revolutionary changes that matter in the lives of pupils; it is the awkward, marginal decisions, the day-to-day politics of the job. Cardinal de Retz said of Richelieu: "He could distinguish better than anyone between the bad and the worse, between the good and the better, a great quality in a minister." It is a great quality in a headmaster too. But in other respects Richelieu is not a good model. Love of grandeur and *raison d'état* are temptations that a headmaster ought to resist. His success should be measured in the lives of his pupils and in the developing careers of his staff. If he is successful both pupils and colleagues will have been given a chance to grow. Forget the new building, the undistinguished portrait in the Hall and the reputation gathering myth as the truth recedes – the real test of a headmaster's success is what the pupils he recruits and the young men he appoints are doing twenty years later.

Unfortunately the pressures on a headmaster to achieve a more immediate and striking success can be very great. All I can say about the experience of what appears to be success is that it makes it easier to resist that pressure. Being well-known frees you from the necessity to prove your head-magisterial virility every five minutes. The achievement of pseudo-success provides the opportunity for the pursuits of the real thing.'[12]

165

15

Looking Back

Forty years on, when afar and asunder,
*   Parted are those who are singing today,*
When you look back, and forgetfully wonder
*   What you were like in your work and your play,*
Then it may be, there will often come o'er you,
*   Glimpses of notes like the catch of a song –*
Visions of boyhood shall float them before you,
*   Echoes of dreamland shall bear them along.*

Because I have been associated with schools for so many years, people often assume that I can give an authoritative opinion on the choice of school for their children. I cannot. All that I have learnt over the years is that there are a great many questions that should be asked.

First, why do parents wish to send their children to boarding-school, and are they achieving the best for their children by so doing? The last person to be consulted is often the child himself, who may have very strong views on the subject. C. R. Nevinson was at Uppingham at the time of the Boer War, and said in his autobiography:

'I had no wish to go to any such school at all, but nevertheless Uppingham did seem to be the best. Since then I have often wondered what the worst was like. No qualms of mine gave me an inkling of the horrors I was to undergo . . . the brutality and bestiality in the dormitories made life a hell on earth. An apathy settled on me. I withered. I learned nothing: I did nothing. I was kicked, hounded, caned, flogged, hairbrushed, morning, noon and night. The more I suffered, the less I cared. The longer I stayed, the harder I grew.'[2]

In spite of Nevinson's strictures, boarding-schools at that time were a necessity; education in the sense of attending school, rather than being taught by a tutor at home, was rarely available within easy travelling distance. The early boarding-schools followed the pattern set by the medieval monasteries which held the monopoly of education in the Middle Ages. With the world-wide expansion of the Victorian empire, diplomats, civil servants, commercial magnates, civil engineers, missionaries and Service officers came to rely on boarding-schools at home for the education of their children. Schools multiplied at an alarming rate, and although the ranks have thinned a little, there is still a vast choice for those who can afford it – each one differing from the others. It is the parents' responsibility to choose the correct school for each child.

What is meant by education? John rightly emphasises that its primary aim is to develop independence of mind. Education should teach children to stand by their convictions. Boys and girls must be taught to evaluate all the information available on a particular topic and to form their own judgment, which may or may not accord with the 'official' view; and having done so, they must be prepared to modify their opinion in the light of further information and experience.

Any system of communal education teaches a child to be tolerant of others, but the effects are emphasised in a boarding-school environment. Children will learn to live in close community with others and to work together. They will be confronted at an early age with jealousy and envy, and will have to learn to control these emotions in themselves, and to withstand being damaged by them in others.

A boy tries to emulate his father, a girl her mother; but no one parent can possess all the qualities of an ideal exemplar. Any school offers a wide range of models for the child to emulate, but in the confines of a boarding-school the influences – both good and bad – will be far stronger. Living in such close proximity to other people, a child should develop an increased awareness and appreciation. The school should try to extend this, to involve first the local environment, and beyond it the world as a whole.

Many parents are inclined to look first at a school's academic record. If there were such a place as the ideal school, fulfilling each and every requirement, I would put passing exams at the bottom of the list. Of course it is important: there has to be an objective standard against which a pupil's ability can be measured – an engineer unable to do simple arithmetic would be an absolute disaster. Critics argue that while some people have the ability to pass exams, others, who do not, are unfairly handicapped: but surely the implication of this is that some individuals will react to the stress and challenges of life by producing their best and others their worst. Exams can not only determine candidates' academic knowledge, but also pinpoint those with strength of character, an essential ingredient for success. Some people claim that if only they had worked they would have obtained a First at 'Oxbridge': Jimmy James used to point out that the 'if only' is what matters. Many have intelligence, but few have the determination to work really hard.

At the same time, the specialisation demanded by the present exam system is too severe and occurs at too early an age. It is increasingly difficult for children to acquire the breadth of knowledge and skills essential to education. Perhaps the Scottish 'Leaving Certificate' and the Continental 'Baccalaureate', with their wide variety of subjects, provide a truer education than England's 'A'-level system with passes in three subjects, perhaps only two, sufficient for university entrance.

How can schools fulfil the needs of all their children? I am taking it for granted that in a sound school the major subjects will be well taught. Beyond this, any attempt to provide a wide choice must be governed by the school's resources. If a school tries to teach half a dozen modern languages seriously and well, it may not only run into financial embarrassment but may put an impossible strain on the masters and the timetable. A school offering three or four languages may be more realistic in its approach and more successful in its teaching than one offering a tempting choice of six. But any well-founded curriculum should be balanced in its emphasis: Science as well as Arts, 'Theory' as well as 'Practical'.

On a recent visit touring Australian schools, we were greatly impressed by the inclusion of practical as well as 'pure' academic subjects. They were all taken equally seriously, neither 'side' being considered inferior. Well aware that the future of their country lies largely in industry, all the Australian schools we visited, both independent and state, prepared children to work in an industrial society. Expensive modern machinery and precision electrical equipment were part and parcel of the whole range of general education. Science properly taught can be a humane subject, and can constitute a very positive education; acceptance of this was prevalent. The same cannot be said for the majority of British private schools.

It is, however, in the extra-curricular subjects that a good school stands out from the merely adequate. Once again, their effectiveness depends on the enthusiasm of the masters in charge. It is this very enthusiasm, this willingness to put in extra hours in the evenings or at weekends, usually unpaid, that is the essential element in education, and can win a response from what may at first appear unpromising material. Glancing at some of the prospectuses from independent schools I am frequently confronted with long lists of up to forty different out-of-school activities. These may range from stamp-collecting through photography and model-making to such esoteric delights as cordon bleu cookery, wine-tasting and madrigals. On the surface, life need never be dull for an enterprising young man at such a school, but in practice too wide a choice can never be staffed adequately. Ask how often these splendid activities can be enjoyed: a sailing club which can only meet once a term will quickly disintegrate from lack of interest. A school should not build up an exaggerated list of interests to attract prospective parents, to the detriment of the boys concerned.

What are the external resources on which the school can draw? A well-placed school can call upon as many outside speakers as the timetable's demands permit and the staff's imagination suggests. Its locality is important here. Well-known speakers are in great demand, and so find it easier to accept commitments in or near large towns with good rail services. The debt owed by schools to such men and women is very great (at the most they get their expenses, and they are often out-of-pocket through their own generosity). Westminster, situated in the heart of London, in the shadow of Parliament, is the best example I know of a school which nearly every lecturer will find it easy to visit. So much can be gained from 'outside' lectures that it is well worth prospective parents asking for a list of the previous year's speakers. Lecturers range from politicians, trade-unionists, university dons, poets, philosophers, astronomers, moral theologians and lawyers, to Communists, supporters of euthanasia and family planning, exponents of extra-sensory perception, and many others. An erudite visitor may be asked to act as principal speaker in a school debate.

Most schools have a debating society, and these can be excellent in giving a student the chance to gain confidence by expressing an argument clearly and learning to defend his views in public. It is also very good practice in learning to see both sides of the question. Careful, if discreet, control by the staff will ensure that the platform is not used to parade the eccentricities of a few, but rather the sincere and well-founded opinions of many.

Ask, too, what opportunity the school provides for increasing a child's awareness of the environment by involving him in community service. Pupils can shop for the elderly, help in local schools for the physically or mentally handicapped, visit the sick, perhaps even give up part of their holiday to entertaining the handicapped as guests of the school. The spread of such activities in recent years may be responsible for teenagers' growing awareness of other people's needs. I have known many boys and girls who, after leaving school, went at their own expense to the 'Third World', and there lived in conditions of considerable discomfort, because they wanted to give positive help. Such social awareness cannot be taught – it can only be learnt by experience and by example. Seniors and staff who have been associated with such work can pass on what they have gained to younger pupils eager to emulate them – we learn from other people's attitudes as expressed by their actions – rather than by what they say.

The benefit of example is particularly important with regard to school rules. Junior pupils will disregard rules openly broken by the seniors, and seniors will respond far more readily to being trusted by the staff than to having any number of official regulations imposed on them. Parents should ask to see a copy of the school rules and draw their own conclusions. I know of schools which have a hundred or more rules and petty regulations. Some schools only issue their rules to the teaching staff and pupils, and I even knew one school which gave copies to the staff alone. The principle should be to have as few rules as possible, and only those which can be seen to make sense. 'Taps must be turned off after use' was Rule 150 in a West Country school – something hardly worth being enshrined in the school rule-book.

Parents are often embarrassed about bringing up the subject of religion. How seriously do schools put into practice their (often sanctimonious) claims in the Public Schools' Year Book? In an increasingly secular age, should they in fact be centres of religious belief? The great Roman Catholic establishments, such as those

170

run by the Benedictines and the Jesuits, will clearly emphasise the practice and teaching of the faith. In other public schools it is the influence and convictions of the headmaster and staff that count; although the Education Act of 1944 laid down certain minimum requirements for religious teaching, a modern school may provide anything from 'cosy chats' about comparative religion, to the four Church services and three Sunday sermons of the Victorian era. If a school takes its religious teaching seriously, its Governing Body must ask more searching questions of a prospective headmaster than 'Are you C. of E.?' – and it could be argued that headmasters should ask similar questions when appointing staff. Agnostic headmasters, staff and parents usually accept that the ethical and moral standards taught by the great religions of the world are potent in the development of character. Proselytising is unnecessary – example is essential. Church or Chapel services, and House prayers, should either be taken by those who believe in what they are doing, or omitted altogether. Nobody is quicker than a schoolboy in spotting hypocrisy or humbug.

What place does the school give to tradition in the liturgy it uses? Boys are far more traditional than they would perhaps admit. Westminster has compulsory morning service in the Abbey, and John once decided to modernise the service by praying spontaneously about present-day problems. As he was walking through the crowded cloisters after the service, he heard one of the scholars say to a friend: 'I don't mind being compelled to listen to Cranmer, but not to the bees in the Head Master's bonnet.' In the majority of English schools 'traditional services' mean 'Church of England', and provided they are taken by those who believe in what they are doing, such services can be of great value to students.

I feel myself that services should rarely be compulsory. However, the alternative should not be an extra hour in bed, but rather a lecture or discussion about some topic that helps to throw light on the human predicament. Students should be given every opportunity to become aware of God – but never coerced.

Is the school single-sex, co-educational, or mixed in the senior forms? Which type of education is best suited to your child? Some headmasters say that introducing girls into a traditionally male school can have the effect of making the senior boys less gauche. On the other hand, there can be no doubt that to board boys and girls together in the same House is to set up enormous stresses at a time in their life when they are least well equipped to deal with them.

In considering a school, parents must bear in mind the fact that times have changed since their own schooldays, and that their children will have been influenced by contemporary views – moral or otherwise – expressed continually in books and magazines, films and the media.

Ask above all whether a boarding-school is the right choice for your child. Whatever its advantages – and there are many – it is an unnatural environment, and to send children to boarding-school breaks up family life for the greater part of their most turbulent yet formative years. They will be away from home for two-thirds of the year, and it is the school, rather than their parents, which will teach them the principles of life – no way to promote family unity, which depends on the sharing of fundamental beliefs. Many parents, of course, are happy to abrogate their responsibilities, but I am describing an ideal family, whose members spend some part of each day together, and this may be as rare as an ideal school. If your home is stable and happy, and there is a well-balanced day school in easy reach, your child may develop best as a day pupil. Boarding-schools, too, take day pupils, and their boarders can be enriched by the experience of visiting the homes of day children. Some children are temperamentally incapable of fitting into boarding-school life. They are often extremely sensitive, and any attempt to 'toughen them up' by forcing them to board can cause utter misery. At the same time, boarding-school has a lot to offer them in the way of continuity and stability. For such a child, being a day pupil at a boarding-school may be the best solution.

Parents often feel over-awed and diffident about asking questions, but an interview with headmaster, housemaster or registrar is a far better guide to the school than the prospectus, which is after all designed to sell a product. It is no exaggeration to say that the decision parents take will have a profound effect on their child's future life – and from the point of view of investment, public-school fees are likely to be their largest single expenditure apart from buying their home. It would indeed be foolish to buy a house without a thorough survey. Ask as many questions as you can, and make them searching ones.

Ask about the school's academic work. Ask about Games: are they compulsory or voluntary? If your child is a poor performer, will he still have the opportunity to play, and if so, how often? I have frequently seen non-athletic boys plodding round a set course, as there were no facilities for them to join a team game. If your child hates the thought of Games and would rather take a bracing walk, will he be catered for? Ask about spare-time activities. Are there any holiday expeditions? Ask about the school's religious bias. Are there facilities for other denominations, including non-Christians? Is there any restriction on the numbers of such children admitted to the school?

How much contact do children have with the staff out of school hours? Are they, for instance, invited to the staff's homes for meals? Masters' wives may have a very important influence on the children. A few years ago, I met an elderly couple. The husband had just been appointed chaplain to a well-known girls' school. During their first year they kept open house every weekend for any girl who wanted to come and relax in a home environment. The door was never closed to anyone at any time. When preparations were being made for a Christmas party, the Head Mistress held a common-room meeting to discuss it with the staff. The chaplain asked whether his wife was expected to wear a long or short dress. 'Your wife is not invited,' said the Head Mistress, 'she is not a member of the staff.' The chaplain and his wife were Christian and forgiving enough to decide that he should attend the party alone – though I know that he went with a heavy heart. He said to me that he could never have done this specialised job without his wife's continual help.

What about discipline? No parent can expect a school that practises corporal punishment to make an exception for their child; if they object to corporal punishment, they must find a school which shares their opinion. Fortunately, in my view, the majority of British public schools have now largely abandoned this practice. Assuming parents do accept corporal punishment as a form of discipline, they should still ask who is allowed to beat pupils and, if junior staff or monitors have the right to do so, what record is kept? Ask, too, what safeguards there are against excessive violence.

Bullying, smoking, drinking and drug-taking amongst the pupils are topics where the questioner must tread warily. Every headmaster is going to defend his school, but it is probably true to say that an outright denial that any or all of these practices take place merely means that a headmaster is deceiving himself. Wherever a group of children live for long periods in a confined society, there will be a tendency for some bullying to occur. Parents should ask what precautions are taken against bullying, and what procedure is followed if cases come to light. The problem of smoking is particularly difficult. Many masters smoke, and it is probably too much to expect them to stop; but I feel they can reasonably be asked to refrain when they are actually with their students, whether in the classroom or at a private tutorial in their study. Both smoking and drinking can kill, the difference being that smoking has a cumulative effect. A 'moderate' smoker has an increased chance of dying from lung cancer or heart disease – a 'moderate' drinker does not diminish his life expectancy. However good the masters' example, some boys will still smoke. What is the school's attitude?

Drug-taking, too, can certainly cause bodily harm, but above and beyond this, it is illegal. A school that fails to deal adequately with drug-takers encourages contempt for the law as well as for physical health. It is highly unlikely that there is any school which has not at one time or another been involved with drugs. Parents should ask outright what the official school view is, and particularly whether a drug provider or dealer is instantly expelled. Does the school try positively to educate students in the risks of smoking, drinking and drug abuse? Without this education it is difficult for the students to understand the risks that they are taking.

Ask how much privacy is available. At what age does a pupil have a study? Is it shared, and if so with how many? What is the position with regard to exeats? Are there facilities for weekly boarding? (Bear in mind that weekly-boarding fees are likely to be identical with full boarding, as the cost to the school in teaching, domestic staff and accommodation is the same.)

In addition to these questions, devise some sort of personal check list, always remembering that it is your child who will be the pupil, and that what would suit you may not be appropriate for your son or daughter. Remember, too, that schools change. The fact that a father was happy at one particular school does not necessarily mean that his son will be, even if father and son are temperamentally the same. The reverse may also be true. A 'poor' school, given a different staff and a conscientious headmaster, may over the years become a 'good' school. The practice of entering a child for a particular public school at birth may be necessary because of the pressure on places, but it does prejudge the questions my hypothetical parents have been asking. Never regard an early decision as unalterable. One way round this is to put the child's name down for several schools, thus ensuring a choice.

Individual Houses within a school reflect the temperament of their housemaster and this, perhaps even more than that of the headmaster, will have an enormous influence on a child's life. Parents will therefore need to choose a House as well as a school, and a good school will give them every opportunity to do so.

One other general point to bear in mind is whether a school is so governed by tradition as to turn its pupils into total conformists – of whom Colonel Blimp is the supreme example. The opposite danger, of course, is the possibility that state schools may in the end be so controlled as to turn out robots.

Finally, when the choice has been made, and the child has actually started at the school, it is up to the parents to watch his progress. Schooldays may not be the happiest days of one's life, but they should be happier and more fulfilling than is often the case.

Our first, second and third daughters were educated at day schools, but a few years ago Emily, our fourth child, decided that her one desire in life was to go to boarding-school. John and I counted up our pennies, and came to the conclusion that as she maintained that she was grossly unhappy at her day school we should somehow find the means to fulfil her wishes. Certainly her work had deteriorated drastically during the previous months; yet we knew that she had ability. She was thirteen, a good age to change schools. We wanted to choose a boarding-school in easy reach of our own, and eventually we narrowed the choice down to two. One was in the depths of the country, the other in beautiful grounds on the perimeter of a city. Emily was interviewed at both schools, and decided that she would be happy at either. We opted for the second.

Three days after Emily started there, I had a 'phone call from her to say that she was unhappy, and that she had decided to leave the school immediately. I persuaded her to stay on, and emphasised that as she had told her previous school that she was desperately unhappy there, I doubted whether they would offer to have her back. A few hours later the Head Mistress telephoned me:

'Emily has just been to see me: she tells me that she is going to leave on Wednesday if you don't come and collect her before then.' She laughed – perhaps to reassure me. 'Don't worry, Mrs

Rae, girls are often homesick for the first few weeks – they never run away.' She added hastily, 'But have you time to come to see her?'

I told the Head Mistress that I would come to the school immediately and try to persuade Emily to remain, as the chances were that she would carry out her threat.

Emily refused to relent when I saw her, though the Head Mistress was convinced that the drama was ephemeral. She told Emily in front of me that she was being rather hysterical, and that if she calmed down she would settle into the school routine and would soon forget the initial period of unrest. Emily stared blankly ahead, and after a period of silence said clearly and emphatically:

'My mother ran away from school, my father ran away from school, and if I am not allowed to leave before Wednesday, I will follow the family tradition.'

As she promised, Emily left after Assembly on Wednesday morning.

In choosing that school we had made a mistake which might have had a disastrous effect on our daughter. We had forgotten that all our girls suffered from homesickness. Whatever her ostensible reasons at the time, Emily ran away because she needed to be at home.

Thinking that we had learned from our mistake, we asked every possible question before our sons entered their boarding-school. In spite of this, one twin ran away in the middle of his fifth term. Three weeks later his brother insisted on leaving. He discussed this with his headmaster first, on a 'man to man' basis, but he would not change his mind.

I wish I could say that having followed my own advice, I had achieved happy and uncomplicated schooldays for my children. Sadly this was not so – though because of my lack of a settled family life as a child, school was the major influence in my early development, and it would be difficult to find a married couple who have had more experience of boarding-school life than John and I.

A boarding-school really is a world apart. In our early days at Harrow, we belonged to a small, close-knit community which for the most part was varied enough and friendly enough to allow us a normal-seeming life, though still with the tendency to look on the outside world as different.

Headmastering at Taunton and Westminster has increased our loneliness. We have fewer friends and more acquaintances, and the pressures of a largely artificial existence led me to work first among the terminally ill in this country and then among the dying and destitute overseas.

But that – together with my further experiences as a head-master's wife – is another story.

NOTES

1   Lockwood, Edward, *Early Days of Marlborough College*, Simpkin Marshall, London, 1893 (pp 25–6)

2   Nevinson, C. R., *Paint and Prejudice*, Methuen, London, 1937

3   Marchand, Leslie A. (ed.), *In My Hot Youth, Byron's Letters and Journals*, Vol. I, John Murray, London, 1973

4   Lunn, Arnold, *Come What May*, Eyre & Spottiswoode, London, 1940

5   Hollis, Christopher, *Eton*, Hollis & Carter (The Bodley Head), London, 1960 (p 36)

6   Personal letter to Daphne Rae, April 21, 1982, quoted by permission of the writer

7   Rosen, Ismond, *Sexual Deviation*, Oxford University Press, London, 1979 (p 11)

8   Purcell, E. S., *Life of Cardinal Manning*, Macmillan, London, 1895 (p 17)

9   Lunn, Arnold, et al., *Public School Religion*, Faber & Faber, London, 1933 (pp 31–3)

10   Churchill, Winston, *My Early Life*, Odhams Press, London, 1930 (pp 16–7)

11   Drummond, Henry, *Baxter's Second Innings*, London, 1892

12   Rae, John, article published in *Punch*, London, March 11, 1981